In *The Spiritual Warfare Battle Plan* Jennifer rips the mask off the subtle assignments of the enemy to kill, steal, and destroy your life. In the pages of this book you'll learn to discern the wily ways of fifteen of the most common demons that harass, bind, oppress, and otherwise oppose God's will for your life and wage war against your mind and body. I highly recommend this book!

—RYAN LeSTRANGE
AUTHOR, *OVERCOMING SPIRITUAL ATTACK*
FOUNDER AND APOSTLE, IMPACT INTERNATIONAL APOSTOLIC
FELLOWSHIP

Jennifer LeClaire has done it again! Her new book, *The Spiritual Warfare Battle Plan*, exposes fifteen demonic enemies that harass and oppress believers. This masterful work does more than diagnose the problem; it gives a complete strategy for victory. This work is a must-have for every serious Christian.

—RON PHILLIPS
PASTOR, ABBA'S HOUSE
CHATTANOOGA, TENNESSEE

Jennifer LeClaire knocked it out of the park again with *The Spiritual Warfare Battle Plan*. This book is a very timely and must-read for the body of Christ in this hour. The Word says people are destroyed for the lack of knowledge. *The Spiritual Warfare Battle Plan* is a book full of useful knowledge about the plans and schemes of the enemy. This book is very informational and educational about the strongholds the enemy wants to bring against you. Jennifer teaches on the demonic spirits of Jezebel, Absalom, Judas, python, and the religious spirit. She teaches us how to come against these spirits in prayer and spiritual warfare. Jennifer also shows us how to identify the different demonic spirits and their actions against us. I encourage every person to read this book and buy this book for others who need to know about spiritual warfare. It is time for the body of Christ to learn how to wage spiritual warfare and live the victorious life that God has called us to live.

—JOE JOE DAWSON
APOSTLE/OVERSEER
ROAR APOSTOLIC NETWORK AND ROAR CHURCH
TEXARKANA, TEXAS

The
SPIRITUAL WARFARE
BATTLE PLAN

The
SPIRITUAL WARFARE
BATTLE
PLAN

JENNIFER LeCLAIRE

CHARISMA
HOUSE

Most CHARISMA HOUSE BOOK GROUP products are available at special quantity discounts for bulk purchase for sales promotions, premiums, fund-raising, and educational needs. For details, write Charisma House Book Group, 600 Rinehart Road, Lake Mary, Florida 32746, or telephone (407) 333-0600.

THE SPIRITUAL WARFARE BATTLE PLAN by Jennifer LeClaire
Published by Charisma House
Charisma Media/Charisma House Book Group
600 Rinehart Road
Lake Mary, Florida 32746
www.charismahouse.com

Unless otherwise noted, all Scripture quotations are taken from the Modern English Version. Copyright © 2014 by Military Bible Association. Used by permission. All rights reserved.

Scripture quotations marked AMPC are from the Amplified Bible, Classic Edition. Copyright © 1954, 1958, 1962, 1964, 1965, 1987 by The Lockman Foundation. Used by permission.

Scripture quotations marked DARBY are from the Darby Translation of the Holy Bible. Public domain.

Scripture quotations marked ESV are from the Holy Bible, English Standard Version. Copyright © 2001 by Crossway Bibles, a division of Good News Publishers. Used by permission.

Scripture quotations marked KJV are from the King James Version of the Bible.

Scripture quotations marked NIV are taken from the Holy Bible, New International Version®, NIV®. Copyright © 1973, 1978, 1984, 2011 by Biblica, Inc.™ Used by permission of Zondervan. All rights reserved worldwide. www.zondervan.com. The "NIV" and "New International Version" are trademarks registered in the United States Patent and Trademark Office by Biblica, Inc.™

Scripture quotations marked NKJV are taken from the New King James Version®. Copyright © 1982 by Thomas Nelson. Used by permission. All rights reserved.

Cover design by Justin Evans

Visit the author's website at www.jenniferleclaire.org.

Library of Congress Cataloging-in-Publication Data:
Names: LeClaire, Jennifer (Jennifer L.), author.
Title: The spiritual warfare battle plan / Jennifer LeClaire.
Description: Lake Mary, Florida : Charisma House, 2017. | Includes
    bibliographical references.
Identifiers: LCCN 2017029171| ISBN 9781629991443 (trade paper) |
ISBN
    9781629991450 (ebook)
Subjects: LCSH: Spiritual warfare.
Classification: LCC BV4509.5 .L4433 2017 | DDC 235/.4--dc23
LC record available at https://lccn.loc.gov/2017029171

The names and identifying details of some people mentioned in this book have been changed to protect the privacy of those individuals.

This book is dedicated to my spiritual warriors at Awakening House of Prayer. Thanks for standing with me through the many attacks outlined in this book. Together we've conquered so many wicked assignments as we stand in unity worshipping Jesus and taking authority over the devil in His mighty name.

CONTENTS

ACKNOWLEDGMENTS

I APPRECIATE SO MUCH the team at Charisma House. Thanks for standing with me as my publisher and co-laborers toward the next great move of God. I'm especially grateful for my Charisma House friends Maureen Eha, Debbie Marrie, Marcos Perez, and Adrienne Gaines for helping me get these prophetic messages out with excellence for the glory of God.

FOREWORD

THE ENEMY COMES to kill, steal, and destroy—but Jesus came to give us abundant life (John 10:10). Over the years I've learned that the enemy comes in many different forms—many different manifestations. From the spirit of fear to the spirit of infirmity to the spirit of death, the devil is crafty and diligent in pursuing his antichrist agenda.

When I wrestled the spirit of death in the United Kingdom, I gained an even deeper understanding of how the kingdom of darkness works. I'll always remember a meeting when a thirty-nine-year-old man, who was sitting on the fourth row and had previously had a stroke, died while I was starting to preach a message on the identity thief. The church was stunned.

What I saw was a strong demonic presence over him. His head was contorting and looked to me like it would almost twist off; his jaw, face, and hands were also contorting. They were drawn up toward his chest in clawlike form. It seemed every muscle was at an extreme strain in his body. He was stiff as a board and his eyes were huge and bugged.

I rushed over to him and put my hands on his chest and forehead. I began to bind the demonic power and command his body to be loosed in Jesus's name. The man started to turn blue and struggled to breathe, but he wasn't sweaty. As I was praying he started to turn purple. However, he still had a strong, regular pulse at the beginning, and I had my hand on his heart so I could feel it beating very hard. Soon

I noticed his breathing started to become even more labored. I continued to forbid Satan from attacking him.

His body began to relax a bit. His head started to turn toward us. His lips turned blue then blue-black. I could feel the presence of the spirit of death all around us. I went from binding the spirit of infirmity to binding the spirit of death. Several of us, including the doctor present who was monitoring the man, witnessed his pupils become fixed and dilated, as they do when people are brain dead. And his breathing became much worse. We were told this was "agonal breathing"—the "death rattle"—that can be heard right before and after a person has died and their body is coming to a stop. I knew about this type of breathing because I saw my mother do it when she passed away.

The man stopped breathing. His head turned to the side and a saliva-type fluid started running out of his mouth. I grabbed some tissue and wiped his mouth. His mother shouted out, "He is dead!" I had my hand on his heart the whole time but felt no heartbeat after his head turned toward me. I stepped back realizing he was dead. A sinking, dark feeling came over me, and I could hear a voice saying, "You don't have enough to do it [see him raised from the dead]." I refused to believe that, so I said, "No!" I became very angry and continued to pray even more fervently. I wasn't willing to see this man die, and I knew others were praying and fighting for him.

The doctor who had been standing beside me monitoring everything later told me he was just about to do CPR. But I began to bind the spirit of death and say, "You can't have him!" I began to declare the resurrection life of Jesus Christ over him. Suddenly the man took a huge, deep breath, and his eyes came back into focus and his color started to return. His lips that were blue-black started to regain their natural color. His eyes that had been being fixed and dilated started to move. Then he rolled himself onto his stomach and pushed himself up on his feet without any assistance as if nothing had happened.

His transformation was instantaneous. We were all in shock at how fast it happened. He began to ask why everyone was staring at him. His mom then began to scream, "He can talk!" As it turns out, after a stroke he had had the year before, the man could say only yes and no. But now he could speak fine.

We tried to get him to sit in a chair, but he wanted to stand. He looked rather vacant at first. As he stood, I turned him toward me and pulled him into my chest—like a hug—and declared a full impartation of life. He let go and then embraced me again. I continued to pray and break off the enemy's assignment against him.

That wrestling match with death was intense, and most of us will never have to wage that kind of warfare—but we are in a war. You may be wrestling fear. You may be battling rejection. Some of you may be fighting with trauma, witchcraft, or python or Leviathan spirits. The devil doesn't have new tricks, but he is strategic in whispering vain imaginations to our souls, developing strongholds in our minds, and oppressing us with his lies.

Jennifer's book exposes some of the most common—yet unnoticed—strategies and tactics of demon powers to ruin God's best-laid plans for your life. In the pages of *The Spiritual Warfare Battle Plan* you will find truth that sets you free. You'll recognize the lies that have held you back from God's abundant life. You'll gain courage to bind the strongman in Jesus's name. You'll be equipped to win whatever unseen force you are wrestling with for His glory.

This book is for you and will take you to a whole new level.

—ROBBY DAWKINS
EVANGELIST, FOUNDING PASTOR, THE VINEYARD CHURCH
AURORA, ILLINOIS

INTRODUCTION

WHEN I GOT saved, I thought I'd spend my life walking beside still waters and lying down in green pastures. I had no idea embracing Jesus as the captain of my salvation (Heb. 2:10, KJV) meant I was enlisting as a soldier in the army of God. I didn't understand how much Satan hated me and how his minions would work to oppose God's will in my life. I knew nothing about the wiles of the enemy, the whole armor of God, or the weapons of my warfare—and my ignorance did not stop the devil from attacking.

I've since learned that believers are soldiers (Phil. 2:25) and Jesus did not come to bring peace but a sword (Matt. 10:34). I've discovered that I'm more than a conqueror in Christ (Rom. 8:37), which also tells me ungodly and unseen forces are trying to conquer me. I've come to understand the devil is under my feet (Rom. 16:20) because Jesus is the head and we're His body. I've grasped that no weapon formed against me will prosper (Isa. 54:17)—but that weapons do form and the enemy uses them to attack.

Unfortunately, I was beat up and beaten down a number of times before I gained this understanding. I found out the hard way that the wicked one introduces vain imaginations that can damage my soul. I discerned after many spiritual skirmishes what the apostle Paul taught: "For though we walk in the flesh, we do not war according to the flesh. For the weapons of our warfare are not carnal, but mighty through God to the pulling down of strongholds" (2 Cor. 10:3–4).

Keep this truth in mind as you read the pages of this book: the enemy comes to kill, steal, and destroy (John 10:10). Every demon has the same mission. How they go about it—their strategies and tactics—are different. A spirit of fear attacks your faith, for example, while a spirit of rejection attacks your identity. A spirit of infirmity attacks your health while a spirit of witchcraft more often attacks your mind.

We are not rendered powerless. The apostle Paul gives us instructions for war in Ephesians 6:

> Finally, my brothers, be strong in the Lord and in the power of His might. Put on the whole armor of God that you may be able to stand against the schemes of the devil. For our fight is not against flesh and blood, but against principalities, against powers, against the rulers of the darkness of this world, and against spiritual forces of evil in the heavenly places. Therefore take up the whole armor of God that you may be able to resist in the evil day, and having done all, to stand. Stand therefore, having your waist girded with truth, having put on the breastplate of righteousness, having your feet fitted with the readiness of the gospel of peace, and above all, taking the shield of faith, with which you will be able to extinguish all the fiery arrows of the evil one. Take the helmet of salvation and the sword of the Spirit, which is the word of God.
> —EPHESIANS 6:10–17

ISN'T SATAN ALREADY DEFEATED?

Many sincere believers argue that Jesus defeated the principalities and powers of which Paul speaks and there is no longer any need for us to fight against hosts of wickedness. It is indeed true that Colossians 2:15 declares, "And having spoiled principalities and powers, he made a shew of them openly, triumphing over them in it" (KJV). The context of this verse, however, is not spiritual warfare; rather, Paul was writing of Satan's power over us. The only power Satan has over a believer is the power we give him through our thoughts, words, and actions.

Moreover, Paul warns us not to be ignorant of the devil's devices (2 Cor. 2:11). Peter admonishes us to "be sober and watchful, because your adversary the devil walks around as a roaring lion, seeking whom he may devour. Resist him firmly in the faith, knowing that the same afflictions are experienced by your brotherhood throughout the world" (1 Pet. 5:8–9). And Paul told Timothy to "fight the good fight of faith" (1 Tim. 6:12).

We know Paul personally wrestled the beast at Ephesus (1 Cor. 15:32). He wasn't wrestling against boars or lions or bears, as some claim. He was fighting with spirits operating through people—and those spirits wanted him dead. I think about the time Jews came from Antioch and Iconium and stirred up a crowd against the apostle. They stoned him and dragged him outside the city, thinking he was dead (Acts 14:19). Clearly a wicked spirit was motivating those Jews to commit such a heinous act.

When in the midst of a spiritual battle—whether in our personal lives or our families or even when contending for revival in our cities and awakening in our nation—many sincere believers tend to petition God to rise up and take action against the enemy. Here's the problem: when it comes to matters of spiritual warfare, God is not the one who needs to wake up and rise up. We do. Sure, we can petition God to break in with light or ask Him to dispatch His warring angels, but ultimately He has given us authority over the enemy.

Yes, legally Jesus defeated the enemy on the cross, yet we see in the Bible scripture after scripture revealing that the enemy still influences the hearts and minds of men. Look around you and you will see the reality of spiritual warfare manifesting in your midst. People are getting kidnapped, raped, and murdered, and even committing suicide. Divorce and child abuse are running rampant in our society. Persecution against Christians and Jews is rising. Sin is raging in the church and in the world. Clearly there's a devil on the loose.

A literal onslaught of principalities, powers, rulers of the darkness of this age, and spiritual hosts of wickedness in heavenly places is working overtime to fulfill Satan's mission. Jesus Himself warned us about the enemy's tactics. Jesus called Satan "the prince of this world" (John 12:31, kjv). Our mission is to get instructions from the Holy Spirit as we worship and wait on the Lord; run to the battle line with our eyes wide open, fully awake to what's happening in the spiritual realm; and enforce Christ's victory over the devil He defeated. Victory belongs to us when we follow the Holy Spirit's battle plan.

YOU HAVE TO EXERCISE YOUR GOD-GIVEN AUTHORITY

While some believers deny the reality of spiritual warfare, others are convinced there is a spiritual battle raging—but based on 2 Chronicles 20:15 and 1 Samuel 17:47, they believe the battle is the Lord's. Ultimately it's true that the battle is the Lord's, but Jeremiah 51:20 is also true: "He says: You are My battle-ax and weapon of war: for with you I will break in pieces the nations, and with you I will destroy kingdoms." We must discern, then, when our worship is our warfare and when we have to run to the battle line and take out our Goliaths. Either way, God is helping us.

Other precious believers want their pastor or some intercessor to fight their battles for them. People have literally tried to hire me to fight Jezebel spirits for them. Still others seem to think God is asleep and if they could just cry out loud enough to wake Him up, they would find deliverance from the spiritual enemies that are sorely oppressing them.

It's true that David often cried out for God to "wake up," but David's cries for the Lord to awaken were just his humble way of showing his utter dependence upon God in the face of his enemies. What's more, David was literally wrestling against flesh and blood and did not have the revelation Paul did about the spiritual army of demons that rise up against God's people behind the scenes. He didn't have Christ's authority to bind the enemy's power in the spirit realm (Matt. 16:19). This authority didn't come to believers until after Christ defeated Satan on the cross.

Here's the bottom line: you can beg God to arise and scatter His enemies all day long (Ps. 68:1), but God already has done everything He's going to do about the devil until Jesus returns to throw him into prison for a thousand years. Christ gave us His authority, and we need to wake up to that reality and start enforcing Christ's victory in this age.

There are entire volumes written on the believer's authority, but let me give you just a couple of scriptures to remind you of the power at your disposal in Jesus. First, God raised Christ from the dead by the power of the Holy Spirit and seated Him at His right hand in heavenly places, "far above all principalities, and power, and might, and dominion, and every name that is named, not only in this age but also in that which is to come. And He put all things in subjection under His feet and made Him the head over all things for the church, which is His body, the fullness of Him who fills all things in all ways" (Eph. 1:21–23).

We also are seated with Christ in heavenly places (Eph. 2:6, ESV). And Jesus has given us, His disciples, authority over demons. We see this for the first time in Matthew 10:1: "He called His twelve disciples to Him and gave them authority over unclean spirits, to cast them out, and to heal all kinds of sickness and all kinds of disease." Before His ascension to heaven, Jesus also said, "In My name they will cast out demons; they will speak with new tongues; they will take up serpents; if they drink any deadly thing, it will not hurt them; they will lay hands on the sick, and they will recover" (Mark 16:17–18). And in Luke 10:19 Jesus says, "Look, I give you authority to trample on serpents and scorpions, and over all the power of the enemy. And nothing shall by any means hurt you."

KNOW YOUR ENEMY

There are thousands of demons that can and do attack believers every day. We live in a dark world that is growing darker. But Satan is strategic. His army is highly organized, and he is sending specific spirits against believers to derail them from their kingdom purpose. Some of those spirits are low-level demons that seek to keep believers from rising up. Others are high-level principalities that attack believers who are using violent faith to advance God's kingdom.

Ephesians 6:12 tells us, "For our fight is not against flesh and blood, but against principalities, against powers, against the rulers of the darkness of this world, and against spiritual forces of evil in the heavenly places." The word *principalities* in this verse comes from the Greek word *archē*. It refers to "the first place, principality, rule, magistracy" and speaks of "angels and demons." [1] Vine's expository dictionary reveals that it is used of "supramundane beings who exercise rule." [2]

These are high-level demons—so high-level, in fact, that an angel needed help from an archangel to break through. Remember Daniel's encounter:

> But then a hand touched me, which set me on my knees and on the palms of my hands. He said to me, "O Daniel, a man greatly beloved, understand the words that I speak to you, and stand upright, for I have been sent to you now." And when he had spoken this word to me, I stood trembling. Then he said to me, "Do not be afraid, Daniel. For from the first day that you set your heart to understand this and to humble yourself before your God, your words were heard, and I have come because of your words. But the prince of the kingdom of Persia withstood me for twenty-one days. So Michael, one of the chief princes, came to help me, for I had been left there with the kings of Persia."
>
> —DANIEL 10:10–13

Principalities are like the CEOs or five-star generals of the demonic realm. They report directly to Satan himself and set themselves over nations and territories.

Powers are the next level. These are like the colonels in the army. The Greek word translated "powers" in Ephesians 6:12 is *exousia*, which refers to "the leading and more powerful among created beings superior to main, spiritual potentates." It also means "power, authority, weight, especially: moral authority, influence." [3] Jesus delegated His power to us and assured us that we have authority over all the power of the enemy (Luke 10:19). The only authority a power has in your life is the power you give it through your thoughts, words, and actions.

The Greek word for wickedness in this verse is *ponēria*, which means unrighteousness, wickedness, greed, fornication, covetousness, and malice.[4] Merriam-Webster's dictionary defines malice as "desire to cause pain, injury, or distress to another" or "intent to commit an unlawful act or cause harm without legal justification or excuse."[5] You may have had some run-ins with spiritual wickedness in heavenly places in your personal spiritual warfare.

The *rulers* in Paul's phrase "rulers of the darkness of this world" comes from the Greek word *kosmokratōr*, which means "lord of the world, prince of this age."[6] But what is this darkness over which they rule? "Darkness" in Ephesians 6:12 comes from the Greek word *skotos*. It can mean darkness, as in the darkness of night. But in this context it means "of ignorance respecting divine things and human duties, and the accompanying ungodliness and immorality, together with their consequent misery in hell." It also means "persons in whom darkness becomes visible and holds sway."[7]

OPEN OUR EYES, LORD!

It has been said that we don't know what we don't know, but it's just as true that we can't see what we can't see. Sometimes the enemy has so clouded our vision that we need God to break in with light—to open our eyes wide so we can see the supernatural events unfolding behind the natural scenes.

Although we walk by faith and not by sight (2 Cor. 5:7), sometimes God will choose to let us see something supernatural to bolster our faith—or just to get our attention when we're going astray.

When God opens our eyes, it may be in the form of a

prophetic dream, a vision, a trance, or even what feels like a real-life experience in heaven or hell. Although we should not seek supernatural experiences for the sake of seeking supernatural experiences—we should seek God and trust that He will give us what we need—there's nothing wrong with crying out to God to open our eyes when we sense we aren't seeing what He really wants us to see.

In Elisha's day the king of Syria was warring against Israel. The prophet Elisha gave the Israelites a marked advantage—he was able to hear the words Syria's king spoke in his bedroom and relayed them to the king of Israel (2 Kings 6:12). The Syrian king wanted Elisha stopped and sent out horses and chariots and a great army to fetch him. When he saw that the Syrian army surrounded the city, Elisha's servant got scared.

> And his servant said to him, "Alas, my master! What will we do?" And he said, "Do not be afraid, for there are more with us than with them." Then Elisha prayed, "LORD, open his eyes and let him see." So the LORD opened the eyes of the young man, and he saw that the mountain was full of horses and chariots of fire surrounding Elisha.
>
> —2 KINGS 6:15–17

What confidence Elisha's servant must have gained—not just in that moment but throughout his walk with the Lord. And that brings me to Paul's prayer for the church at Ephesus, which is something I would suggest praying over yourself daily. In this prayer Paul asks the Lord to open the believers' eyes for a specific purpose—a purpose that is sure to spark faith in your soul and spirit:

Therefore I also, after hearing of your faith in the Lord Jesus and your love toward all the saints, do not cease giving thanks for you, mentioning you in my prayers, so that the God of our Lord Jesus Christ, the Father of glory, may give you the Spirit of wisdom and revelation in the knowledge of Him, that the eyes of your understanding may be enlightened, that you may know what is the hope of His calling and what are the riches of the glory of His inheritance among the saints, and what is the surpassing greatness of His power toward us who believe, according to the working of His mighty power.

—EPHESIANS 1:15–19

As you read through the chapters of this book, my prayer is that you will gain discernment to identify spirits opposing your life—and the lives of those you love—and develop spiritual skills to battle back. We will unmask the strategies and operations of fifteen spirits that frequently combat believers in our generation. Although the list of demons that could attack a believer is long, the ones addressed here will put you well on your way to conquering the most insidious hidden enemies. Each chapter will provide tools for identifying the root issue by recognizing the fruit the spirit often brings, as well as a strategy to overcome its attack. Because the mission of this book is to help you walk in freedom, I include prayer starters you can use to begin to break the spirits' hold. You will notice that every prayer contains an element of repentance because it is important that you always repent before engaging the enemy.

As you read this book, I also hope you will recognize how to guard yourself from being used by the enemy. Most of the spirits we will discuss can work through you to attack others.

Rather than merely pointing fingers at people in whom you see these spirits operating, be careful to examine your own life and heart for any of the tendencies these spirits manifest in believers. Ultimately you can't take authority over the devil when you are acting like the devil.

Spiritual bondage can manifest in many ways, but the good news is that victory can be ours. By walking in our God-given authority, we can effectively do battle and win in warfare.

PART ONE

PRINCIPALITIES THAT PREY ON BELIEVERS

CHAPTER 1

ANTICHRIST SPIRITS' ANTI-ANOINTING AGENDA

IT FELT LIKE I was surrounded on all sides—because I was. Someone operating in a Jezebel spirit infiltrated my ministry at Awakening House of Prayer on a seek-and-destroy mission. A businessman in my community started spreading vicious lies about me based on his vain imaginations and hallucinatory offenses. Then, much like what happened to Paul in Galatians 2:4, false brethren came in unawares to spy out our liberty and reported having had ungodly arguments with me. Those incidents never could have taken place, because I wasn't even in town when they allegedly occurred.

But wait, it doesn't stop there. I got sick repeatedly. I took a major financial hit. My teeth were breaking almost faster than I could get to the dentist. And the property owner with whom I inked a deal to rent ministry space reneged at the last second on the grounds that I'm a woman, which meant the ministry was facing homelessness. This was nuclear warfare.

I didn't need any special discernment to recognize the enemy onslaught raging against me. I discerned spirits of sabotage, Jezebel, religion, and accusation but didn't immediately

THE SPIRITUAL WARFARE BATTLE PLAN

understand that antichrist spirits were organizing the campaign against my life and ministry. My tolerating Jezebel was the open door, and antichrist spirits seized the opportunity to strike.

I didn't recognize the strategies of these demons because I'd never witnessed their maneuvers up close and personal, nor had I studied these wicked forces much. Antichrist spirits are not on most spiritual warriors' demon hit list—but they should be. I am convinced antichrist is a master spirit with dark organizational powers that rallies destructive antichrist forces against unsuspecting believers. Now I know how to fight it.

JOHN'S REPEATED WARNINGS ABOUT ANTICHRIST SPIRITS

Although some argue Pope Francis, President Barack Obama, or President George W. Bush are the biblical Antichrist, these extreme assumptions are a distraction from the real battle at hand. Satan himself is the Antichrist, and he deploys antichrist spirits to attack believers. The antichrist spirits John mentions in his epistles are referred to as *antichristos*. That is the Greek word meaning "the adversary of the Messiah."[1]

"Antichrist" essentially means "anti-anointing," since the Greek word *Christos* is defined as "anointed."[2] The antichrist spirit wants to kill the anointing on your life with an onslaught of coordinated spiritual terror attacks that wear you out. Daniel 7:25 paints a picture of the Antichrist's strategy, and antichrist spirits employ the same tactics: "He shall speak words against the Most High and shall wear out the saints of the Most High and plan to change times and law."

Not to be confused with the Antichrist himself—who is also referred to as the son of perdition in 2 Thessalonians

2:3–4 (KJV), the man of lawlessness doomed for destruction (2 Thess. 2:3, NIV), the dragon in Revelation 12, and the beast in Revelation 13:3–8—antichrist spirits have been roaming the earth for centuries. Antichrist spirits work hard to convince lost souls not to embrace the anointing that sets them free. The atheist and secular humanist movement is growing rapidly as a result. John the Apostle warned about antichrist spirits repeatedly in his epistles. Let's examine those warnings:

> Little children, it is the last hour. As you have heard that the antichrist will come, even now there are many antichrists. By this we know that it is the last hour.
>
> —1 JOHN 2:18

"Even now there are many antichrists." It is certainly a sign of the times, but it's not new. It's just a sign many believers have not learned to discern spiritually. We can see the atheist battles against donning "In God We Trust" on our currency and warring to remove the Ten Commandments from public spaces, but we are slower to recognize the signs of an antichrist spirit's attack against our lives.

> I have written to you, not because you do not know the truth, but because you know it, and because no lie is of the truth. Who is a liar but the one who denies that Jesus is the Christ? Whoever denies the Father and the Son is the antichrist. No one who denies the Son has the Father; the one who confesses the Son has the Father.
>
> —1 JOHN 2:21–23

Antichrist spirits are often behind the deception clouding the minds of those who flat-out deny Christ and those who turn away from Him. Those raised in Christian homes who resist the Lord are deceived by the working of an antichrist spirit. It may seem they followed football or girls or drugs or even a demanding career of some sort, but make no mistake: an antichrist spirit worked on their emotions and reasoning to pull them away from the Father's heart.

> For many imposters (seducers, deceivers, and false leaders) have gone out into the world, men who will not acknowledge (confess, admit) the coming of Jesus Christ (the Messiah) in bodily form. Such a one is the imposter (the seducer, the deceiver, the false leader, the antagonist of Christ) and the antichrist. Look to yourselves (take care) that you may not lose (throw away or destroy) all that we and you have labored for, but that you may [persevere until you] win and receive back a perfect reward [in full].
>
> —2 JOHN 7–8, AMPC

In Matthew 24:24 Jesus warns of the rise of false Christs and false prophets who show great signs and wonders that would deceive many—even some in the church. The New Testament warns repeatedly of false apostles, false prophets, and false teachers. Though they are not specifically mentioned, it is safe to conclude that false evangelists and false pastors also are an unfortunate reality. Paul mentioned that some preach Christ "out of envy and strife" (Phil. 1:15).

Antichrist spirits are operating through false leaders today just as they were in John's day. These false apostles, prophets, evangelists, pastors, and teachers are faking healings, money "miracles," and instant weight-loss "wonders"; preaching perverted gospels; puffing themselves up with dreams they have not had, visions they have not seen, and prophetic words they have not heard; and merchandising the saints in the process. This is one way antichrist spirits are attacking the church within the church. Know the Word of God and the ways of God, and you will not fall for these seductive shenanigans.

BEWARE THE SPIRIT OF THE WORLD

Antichrist spirits reign in the world system. In connection with his exhortation on discerning the antichrist spirit, John makes it clear this anti-anointing spirit is running wild in the world. God did not create the world as a resting place for antichrist spirits, but when Adam and Eve fell, they opened the garden gate—and all the world—to the rule of the Antichrist and the attack of antichrist spirits. Let's look at the apostle's teaching:

> This is how you know the Spirit of God: Every spirit that confesses that Jesus Christ has come in the flesh is from God, and every spirit that does not confess that Jesus Christ has come in the flesh is not from God. This is the spirit of the antichrist, which you have heard is coming and is already in the world. You are of God, little children, and have overcome them, because He who is in you is greater than he who is in the world.
>
> —1 John 4:2–4

We have to be careful not to take this teaching out of context. Surely false prophets can claim Jesus is Lord. That doesn't prove they are working for Christ. If you look closely, the fruit of their ministry will belie their words. At the same time, antichrist spirits are at the core of false religions that offer some other way to heaven besides Christ, the door

(John 10:9). We don't need another testament of Jesus Christ beyond the Bible. We don't need another witness to Jehovah. Buddha and Muhammad can't save anyone.

Jesus defeated the Antichrist and took back the keys to death, hell, and the grave (Rev. 1:18). Christ's followers, then, have authority in His name over antichrist spirits and are not to have any communion with them. But when we let the spirit of the world sway us from taking a strong stance on God's Word, we are ripe for an antichrist attack. We have been warned over and over again to beware of falsehoods and the spirit of the world. Friendship with the world makes you an enemy of God (James 4:4).

Put another way, since antichrist spirits operate in cooperation with the spirit of the world, you are in danger of antichrist spirits influencing you if you fellowship or get into agreement with the world system. The spirit of the world is the spirit that murdered the eleven apostles in the early church and Jesus Christ Himself. Like antichrist spirits, the spirit of the world attacks anyone who names Jesus as Lord.

James urges believers to "keep oneself unstained by the world" (James 1:27). Paul admonishes us not to be "conformed to this world, but be transformed by the renewing of your mind, that you may prove what is the good and acceptable and perfect will of God" (Rom. 12:2). John warns us, "Do not love the world or the things in the world. If anyone loves the world, the love of the Father is not in him" (1 John 2:15).

THE ANTICHRIST SPIRIT'S ARTFUL ATTACK

Antichrist spirits are especially crafty, even artful. Genesis 3:1 says the serpent, the devil, was "more subtle than any beast of the field which the LORD God had made." The Amplified

Bible, Classic Edition calls him "subtle and crafty," while *The Message* describes him as "clever." An antichrist spirit seduced Eve into disobeying God by suggesting falsities about the Almighty.

So subtle is the antichrist spirit's initial attack against your mind that you may not recognize it until after you fall for it—and even then you may not discern it. It takes the truth found in the Word and the anointing of God to break free from an antichrist attack. Genesis reveals clearly how this spirit works through our own reasoning and ambition.

We first see the antichrist spirit as it wiggles its way into the Garden of Eden with a carefully crafted temptation that wears down Eve's thinking concerning her identity in God. The antichrist spirit's weapon of deceptive reasoning ultimately led to the fall of man. Picture the scene in Genesis 3:1–7:

> And he said to the woman, "Has God said, 'You shall not eat of any tree of the garden'?"
>
> And the woman said to the serpent, "We may eat of the fruit from the trees of the garden; but from the fruit of the tree which is in the midst of the garden, God has said, 'You will not eat of it, nor will you touch it, or else you will die.'"
>
> Then the serpent said to the woman, "You surely will not die! For God knows that on the day you eat of it your eyes will be opened and you will be like God, knowing good and evil."
>
> When the woman saw that the tree was good for food, that it was pleasing to the eyes and a tree desirable to make one wise, she took of its fruit and ate; and she gave to her husband with her, and he ate. Then the eyes of both were opened, and they

knew that they were naked. So they sewed fig leaves
together and made coverings for themselves.

God has given us the ability to reason, but He also has
commanded us to obey. An antichrist spirit will attack your
mind so you will reason your way into disobedience. The
antichrist spirit also will attack your identity in Christ, and
this spirit—the spirit of the accuser of the brethren (Rev.
12:10)—will inspire people to rise up against you and lay all
manner of false charges at your feet to wear you out.

The antichrist spirit will slander you, especially if you are
exercising your gifts for the glory of God. The antichrist
spirit wants to stop you from moving in the anointing and
will plague your mind and your life with varied attacks that
aim to shut you down. But remember, greater is He who is
in you than he who is in the world (1 John 4:4).

ANTICHRISTS OPERATING IN SOCIETY

In his book *The Future War of the Church*, Chuck Pierce
points out five areas in which the antichrist system operates.
Antisemitism is an obvious manifestation, and we have discussed the misuse of prophetic gifts. But, Pierce notes, the
antichrist spirit also seeks to oppress women so the image of
God cannot be revealed in its full expression as the body of
Christ labors to fulfill the Great Commission.[3]

Ethnic domination is another manifestation of the antichrist spirit, he explains, that seeks to keep entire people
groups blind to the gospel. A less obvious manifestation of
the antichrist spirit is sexual perversion. Pierce argues that
sexual expressions outside the boundaries of God's original
plan is a sign of lawlessness. Although spirits such as Jezebel
and the lust of the flesh are certainly involved in sexual

perversion, the overarching influence is the rebellious antichrist spirit.[4]

A discerning eye can clearly see the antichrist spirit operating in society. I think of Oklahoma allowing the Ten Commandments monument on the state Capitol lawn. This is the type of event that typically gets radical secular humanists up in arms, with them posting billboards and filing lawsuits aimed at removing any reminder of God and His Son from the public square—and that's exactly what happened. The American Civil Liberties Union immediately sued to have the Ten Commandments monument removed, but the Satanic Temple suggested a compromise.

Operating in an antichrist spirit, the Satanists proposed a seven-foot-tall monument of Baphomet, an idol often found in occult practices. The seven-foot monument features the devil in goat form—half man and half goat. Two children are looking up to him in adoration. The statue encourages children to sit on Lucifer's lap. The antichrist push forced Oklahoma to remove the Ten Commandments so the state didn't have to give equal time to the Satanists, but the statue found a home in Detroit.[5]

Detroit has also emerged as a Muslim stronghold. Islam is an antichrist religion because it rejects Jesus as the only way to salvation. Today, Michigan is home to the first Muslim-majority US city (Hamtramck, located near Detroit), and the state has a growing Muslim community.[6]

It is no surprise that Michigan's economy has struggled, that Detroit is listed as the most dangerous city in America,[7] that drinking water contamination in Flint is making children sick in high numbers,[8] or that HIV among African Americans in Detroit is rising at an alarming rate.[9] Of course, Detroit is not the only antichrist stronghold in the nation. The antichrist spirit is rapidly rising in this hour, and you can expect to see more manifestations in the months and years ahead.

Since the Supreme Court ruled in favor of legalizing same-sex marriage in June 2015, the antichrist spirit has grown bolder. This anti-anointing spirit is working to quench the Holy Spirit, to combat the gospel, and to persecute believers. This is one of the overarching principalities that believers will have to face—and one that will grow stronger until the day of the Lord's return.

Before the Antichrist—Satan—comes on the scene, we will see more and more antichrist spirits rising to push Jesus out of the mainstream. As John the Baptist prepared the way for Jesus's first coming, these demonic forerunners have been voices crying in the wilderness for years, preparing the way for Satan himself with deceiving agendas that target the confused, hurt, and lost.

Indeed, the antichrist agenda will become bolder, and the culture will grow darker in the days ahead. Nevertheless, Jesus is still Lord. Our job is to let our light shine, speak the truth of the gospel in love, and keep our eyes on Jesus, the author and finisher of our faith, so we can rescue people from the kingdom of darkness and escape the prophesied great falling away among the saints.

The late evangelist and pastor David Wilkerson once said this about the antichrist agenda: "You must understand—the Antichrist is not going to suddenly appear on the scene and overwhelm humankind. Rather, his spirit is mysteriously at work now, setting up his kingdom in cold, compromising hearts. And when the Man of Sin finally appears, he will be publicly revealed to a world that is already prepared for him—to hearts his spirit already possesses! Right now we see a growing antichrist sentiment and conduct. But soon this will turn into a flowing stream, and, eventually, a vast ocean. And when the Antichrist finally appears, even many former Christians will welcome him—because their hearts will be of a kindred spirit!"[10]

A PRAYER AGAINST THE ANTICHRIST SPIRIT'S AGENDA IN YOUR LIFE

Maybe your eyes have been opened to the prevalence of antichrist spirits. Before you can take authority over these attacks, you need to make sure you are not in alignment with these demons. This prayer starter will help you come out of agreement with these spirits:

> *Father, I come to You with a heart of repentance for any agreement, alignment, association, covenant, or vow I've formed with antichrist spirits knowingly or unknowingly. Forgive me for the times I have not shared my faith because I was afraid of people.*
>
> *I renounce all generational sin, rejection, and stubbornness against Your plans and kingdom purposes. I repent of all idolatry, worship of false gods, mocking and denying You, unforgiveness toward You, or blaspheming You in my family line. Forgive me, Lord. Forgive us, Lord. Cleanse us from this unrighteousness.*
>
> *I plead the blood of Jesus over myself and my family right now, in Jesus's name. I sever the bands, fetters, and cords of the antichrist spirit. Lord, release me and my family from bondage to antichrist spirits. I stop up all the wicked rivers of antichrist spirits flowing into our lives. I release Your hammer and fire against antichrist spirits. I command spiritual blindness to loose us.*

I bind the voice, lies, whispers, and suggestions of antichrist spirits. I break their yoke over my mind, body, finances, relationships, and every other area of my life. Thank You, Lord, for delivering me from the bonds of antichrist spirits. Increase my discernment and give me strength to stand for You. In Jesus's name, amen.

CHAPTER 2

JEZEBEL GOES FOR THE JUGULAR

I HAVE HAD MY fair share of battles with the spirit of Jezebel. This sapping principality cost me time, money, friends, my health, and my peace of mind—more than once. Others don't get off so easily. I've read horror stories of this spirit splitting up marriages, destroying families, stealing inheritances, and more.

Most of my battles with the Jezebel spirit—a principality that got its name because it displays the characteristics of the wicked Queen Jezebel in the Old Testament and the woman who calls herself a prophetess in the New Testament—have been in the heavenlies. But I have faced fierce battles with this spirit at the ground level. In other words, I've had people under Jezebel's influence try to lead me into idolatry and immorality.

Let me define this spirit before we go further. Jezebel is not a spirit of control and manipulation. There are spirits of control and manipulation that operate in their own right, and Jezebel works with these spirits—or simply with someone's uncrucified flesh—to get to its end game. In other words, someone who is under the influence of a Jezebel spirit often carries or taps into spirits of control and manipulation and will use these tactics to get what they want from you.

Jezebel is a seducing spirit that seeks to tempt God's people into immorality and idolatry. Jesus rips the mask off Jezebel in Revelation 2:18–25:

> The Son of God, who has eyes like a flame of fire, and whose feet are like fine brass, says these things: I know your works, love, service, faith, and your patience, and that your last works are more than the first.
>
> But I have a few things against you: You permit that woman Jezebel, who calls herself a prophetess, to teach and seduce My servants to commit sexual immorality and eat food sacrificed to idols. I gave her time to repent of her sexual immorality, but she did not repent. Look! I will throw her onto a sickbed, and those who commit adultery with her into great tribulation, unless they repent of their deeds. I will put her children to death, and all the churches shall know that I am He who searches the hearts and minds. I will give to each one of you according to your deeds.
>
> Now to you I say, and to the rest in Thyatira, as many as do not have this teaching, who have not known what some call the "depths of Satan," I will put on you no other burden. But hold firmly what you have until I come.

HAND-TO-HAND SPIRITUAL COMBAT

I've had many small skirmishes with people operating in a Jezebel spirit, but most times the spirit has not infiltrated my life on any significant level. My very first experience with Jezebel was a man in a local church who fancied me and started stalking me. He would wait outside my house and suddenly appear at the entry of my condo building. It was super creepy.

I rejected his advances, but he would not relent. Church leadership eventually confronted him, and when he refused to repent he was told not to come back. It turns out I was not the only woman in the congregation he was trying to seduce.

Ironically the second experience with Jezebel at the ground level came at the hands of the same church that helped protect me from the stalking seducer. This church taught about Jezebel ad nauseam. To say they were out of balance is an understatement. Nevertheless, the church was full of Jezebel's fruit. The girls on the worship team were turning up pregnant. Other leaders fell into drunkenness and still others were caught in financial scandals. Those are manifestations of immorality and idolatry.

When I saw Jezebel's stronghold in that church—and when I realized leadership would not deal with the spiritual slime—the Holy Spirit told me to "go in peace." I was persecuted on my way out the door and labeled a Jezebel. That spirit does not like to be identified, especially when it has a stronghold established, and will turn the tables on you. But remember, Jesus said we are not to tolerate Jezebel. It's better to face some persecution in leaving than to face the consequences of tolerating this principality.

The next Jezebel confrontation came from another man who pursued me. I did not want to have anything to do with him, but he was relentless. Finally, I agreed to go out with him and his children to have pizza. Soon enough, he decided I was his wife and started making sexual advances at me. I slammed the door in his face, notified my building security never to let him on the property, cut every other communications tie, and didn't look back. I refused to leave any open door for that spirit to walk through. If the person will not repent, it's best to cut off all ties—including soul ties.

The Bible doesn't use the term *soul tie*, but it is a biblical concept. A soul tie happens when people's souls are knit together in close relationships, as in the case of Jonathan and David (1 Sam. 18:1); during sexual relations when two become one flesh (Eph. 5:31); or when you make vows to or covenants with someone, as described in Numbers 30:2. Soul ties can be healthy with family, but they become unhealthy when sin—or evil spirits—are involved.

Practically speaking, having sex with someone—whether in or out of wedlock—can form a soul tie. Much the same, sharing personal information in confidence with a friend can create a soul tie, as can making a covenant with someone or pledging a vow of loyalty to them. You can even unknowingly make vows with spirits by saying things like "I'll never let anyone hurt me like that again" or "I will always protect my back from now on."

The fourth especially significant encounter with someone operating in a Jezebel spirit came through a woman who had been severely wounded and spiritually abused. She started coming to our ministry, and we had mutual friends. She confessed she was molested, her father was abusive, and just about every church she went to had wronged her.

I took pity on her and determined to help her walk into freedom. But she didn't want to get free. She used her past to manipulate her present. In other words, her game was to make everyone feel sorry for her. I am not even sure her stories were based in reality. She was just looking for a leadership position and a free ride in life to make up for her past traumas.

This experience drained me on every level. I was constantly sick. I started battling depression. I could not sleep. I felt like giving up. My prayer life was affected. My finances were attacked. Jesus said that when you tolerate Jezebel, you will end up on a sickbed with her. It doesn't matter if you discern Jezebel in your midst or not. A lack of discernment is no excuse for tolerating evil. Paul warns us in 2 Corinthians 2:11 not to be ignorant of the devil's devices.

HOW JEZEBEL OPERATES AT THE GROUND LEVEL

I don't believe someone can actually have a spirit of Jezebel in the same way someone has a spirit of fear or a spirit of rejection. I believe that as a principality, Jezebel works to develop strongholds in people's minds such as fear, rejection, apathy, manipulation, and control.

Jezebel clearly seeks to seduce and often works through teaching and prophecy (Rev. 2:20). This spirit seduces the saints into idolatry and immorality. This spirit may use control and manipulation to do it, but ultimately that's not the end game. In fact, ultimately Jezebel's end game is murder. The wages of sin is death, and Jezebel leads people into sin.

Pastors—or anyone, for that matter—who fall into sexual sin are among Jezebel's trophies. If you are doing anything at all for God—and especially if you have a prophetic mandate on your life—Jezebel wants to cut off your voice. If Jezebel can't cut off your voice, it will try to pervert your voice by seducing you to defile yourself by tolerating its activity.

People influenced by a Jezebel spirit target the leader. They usually offer to help where help is desperately needed, either in administration, intercession, or some other area that puts them close to the leader. People in Jezebel's grip make false covenants they don't intend to keep in order to gain position. They will often say, "I will fight with you. I will stand with you. I don't give up easy. No matter what happens, I will have your back." But these are empty promises.

People operating in a Jezebel spirit seem spiritual to outsiders. They talk about their prayer lives and forty-day fasts. They exuberantly share what they see in the spirit realm. They may pray eloquent prayers and prophesy encouraging words to members over in the corner where no one else can hear. They gather people to themselves.

Jezebel's puppets seek to isolate leaders from those who can speak into their lives, especially prophetic people who can identify the spirit influencing them. They pit people against one another in the ministry, and those who threaten them are set up and chased out. They are experts at playing the victim. They want pity.

People influenced by a Jezebel spirit always think they are right. They are never wrong. The problem is always with someone else and never them. If they do repent, it's a false repentance to stay on someone's good side. They may seem humble, but it's false humility stemming from a religious spirit.

People in Jezebel's clutches really feel self-important. Remember, that woman Jezebel called herself a prophetess (Rev. 2:20). Those under Jezebel's influence must have their way—and they manipulate to get it. They will not be held accountable to anyone. If anyone tries to bring accountability, they accuse that person of being a Jezebel.

People with a Jezebel spirit look for those who are hurt and wounded or insecure and become their prophet, teacher, and spiritual guide. They draw people to themselves, who become their eunuchs. They will try to make people feel guilty if they don't bow to their needs. They will say the person isn't operating in the fruit of the Spirit or acting

Christlike as a ploy to make the individual submit to what they want.

Jezebelic people will twist the facts. They have selective memory. They are smooth and slick and will almost convince you they are right. Those flowing in a high-level Jezebel spirit will actually start praying witchcraft prayers against you—praying their own will rather than God's will. They will pray such things as, "Lord, remove that person from that position. That position belongs to me."

I subscribe to the theory of demon possession the late Dr. Lester Sumrall writes about in his classic Demonology and Deliverance series: it starts with regression (people reverting to old behavior patterns) and progressively moves on to possession. I believe this is why Jezebel pressures people's emotions. It wants them to overreact when someone taps into an old, unhealed wound and then gradually find themselves in its bondage.

JEZEBEL'S ROTTEN FRUIT

At the surface level—and from my practical experience dealing with this spirit—the fruit of the Jezebel spirit includes control, manipulation, flattery, strife, defensiveness, pride, dishonesty, ungratefulness, a critical spirit, over-competitiveness, intimidation, super-spiritualism, pushiness, attention-seeking, vengefulness, disapproval, over-ambition, independence, disdain for authority, position-seeking, lust, hunger for power, and a religious spirit. But seeing these traits in people doesn't automatically mean they are influenced by Jezebel. It's dangerous to make a false accusation like that.

Remember, those operating in this spirit are like puppets in this principality's hands, as I explain in my book

Jezebel's Puppets. Jezebel will try to use insecurity, emotional instability, pride, arrogance, manipulation, and control to influence people, and it often preys on people with those characteristics. It's vital that you not have any common ground with this spirit. Again, if you have created unhealthy soul ties, break them. If you've made a vow with any spirit other than the Spirit of God, renounce it. If you are in any kind of relationship with someone operating in a Jezebel spirit and they won't repent, distance yourself. And if you can't distance yourself, at least refuse to bow down to Jezebel's tactics. Remember, you can't bow to the Spirit of Christ and the spirit of Jezebel at the same time.

If you discern a Jezebel spirit in your midst, confront it quickly. Time is not on your side. The longer you wait to confront it, the more damage it can do. What's more, if you tolerate that spirit, Jesus has issues with you. He says in Revelation 2 that if Jezebel doesn't repent, He will throw her on a sickbed and those who commit adultery with her into great tribulation (v. 22).

STOP THROWING JEZEBEL BOMBS

I'm told the first book about Jezebel was published in 1971, though I have not been able to find it in print. There have been plenty of books on this wicked principality since. Still, we keep falling for Jezebel's schemes. We keep making false Jezebel accusations. We keep misunderstanding what Jezebel really is and its ultimate goal. We're quick to throw a Jezebel label on any woman with a strong personality, but it should be noted that men can also operate in a Jezebel spirit, as the examples from my life show. Yet most of the time it operates through women.

I've been part of churches where people are labeled

Jezebels shortly after they walk in the door. They are marked with a scarlet letter as controllers and manipulators who want to get close to the pastor for power and position. In reality, they may be controllers and manipulators, or they may not be. The real controllers and manipulators are more often, in my experience, the ones slinging the misguided Jezebel accusations.

An abusive church leader once said he saw a Jezebel spirit superimposed over my body and that I was in danger of giving myself over to Jezebel if I didn't step in line with his wishes. I was certainly alarmed, so I submitted myself to several pastors outside that church for a thorough examination. One of the pastors asked me a startling question:

"Are you sleeping around?"

"No!" I exclaimed, not understanding why he would ask such a thing.

"Are you leading people away from Jesus?"

"Of course not!" I said.

"Then you aren't operating in a Jezebel spirit."

That set me free and helped me see where the true Jezebel was operating.

Remember Revelation 2:20: "But I have a few things against you: You permit that woman Jezebel, who calls herself a prophetess, to teach and seduce My servants to commit sexual immorality and eat food sacrificed to idols." Along with "false prophet," a Jezebel accusation is one of the most serious fiery darts you can throw at a believer. It implies the person isn't a believer at all but is a fornicator who will not inherit the kingdom of God and a false brother who is purposefully leading people away from Christ for selfish gain.

If you do happen upon people operating in a Jezebel spirit, why not do what Jesus did and give them space to repent? In other words, try to help them get free instead of automatically chasing them out the door and letting the real Jezebels keep running around the church.

A PRAYER THAT HITS JEZEBEL'S JUGULAR

Jezebel is not something you can tear down once and for all, but you can break agreement with it and refuse to tolerate it. Pray the following if you are battling Jezebel, and let the Holy Spirit lead you from here:

> *Father, I thank You for opening my eyes to the subtle manipulations and controlling tactics of Jezebel. Please continue to sharpen my discernment and open my spiritual eyes wider that I might see the offensive operations of this principality coming against my life. I repent for tolerating Jezebel and ask Your forgiveness, in Jesus's name.*
>
> *I decree and declare that Jezebel has no place in me. I ask You to heal my heart of any detected or undetected hurts, wounds, offenses, pains, pride, rejection, rebellion, or any other open door that may have let or could let Jezebel into my life. Help me walk humbly, wisely, and circumspectly, and refuse to engage in activities that attract Jezebel's witchcraft into my life.*
>
> *I renounce all soul ties, affiliations, associations, partnerships, alliances, and covenants with the Jezebel spirit and those under its influence. Sever the ties that bind. Expose the lies that deceive. Confound this spirit and all of its allies. Deliver me from evil.*
>
> *Now I stand against the spirit of Jezebel and its cohorts. I break Jezebel's witchcraft, controlling powers, flatteries, deception, word curses, fearful*

assaults, false accusations, polluted prophetic utterances, subtle seductions, sorceries, intimidations, and other foul operations, in the name of Jesus. Amen.

CHAPTER 3

LEVIATHAN'S TWISTED LIES

WE WERE LIKE brother and sister. We agreed on everything. We ran hard after the will of the Lord. We prayed together. We worshipped together. We warred together. All the while, Leviathan was waiting in the wings to manifest an attack that would drive us apart. I never saw it coming until it happened—and that's often how it is with this bold behemoth.

My brother, we'll call him Jack, got extremely offended because I couldn't immediately pick up the phone when he called as I had done in the past. There was a good reason. Mass renovations were under way at my condo building. My windows were sealed shut with blue film as jackhammers blasted away with deafening noise as they tore off old balconies. I wore ear plugs and pressed through, but taking calls became impossible most of the day.

The pride working in Jack's heart caused him to rise up against me based on a twisted perception that I was rejecting and disrespecting him. I tried to explain over and over again, but the offense hardened his heart and he would not listen to me. Soon I started getting aggressive texts and e-mails with outlandish accusations I could not even wrap my mind around. It was especially hurtful, given how close we were.

He would demand that I call him urgently in one breath, then insist I never call him again in the next breath. It was twisted, schizophrenic behavior.

I knew a wicked spirit was influencing Jack's behavior, but he couldn't see it. A principality was at work on his mind, convincing him I was operating in a foul spirit. I was already in the midst of another serious trial—a trial more severe than his attacks, my blue windows, and the jack-hammer raging in my ears.

There was complete chaos all around me, and I did not know if it would ever end. I tried to keep my mouth shut and my head down, batten down the hatches, and stand in the midst of the storm. He fled the state with bitterness in his heart. Later he repented for the behavior and I embraced him, but the relationship has never been quite the same. Leviathan's residue still influences his mind and, at times, he turns and attacks me.

UNDERSTANDING THIS
FIRE-BREATHING ENEMY

The Leviathan spirit is especially prominent in coastal cities or wherever there are large bodies of water, because it is a water spirit. It manifests strongly in my area of South Florida. But this principality's activity is not restricted to regions marked by oceans, lakes, and rivers. Leviathan works to find an open door in churches and in the lives of individual Christians who attend those churches. Job 41:1 gives us our first look at Leviathan in Scripture: "Can you draw out Leviathan with a hook or snare his tongue with a line which you let down?"

The Hebrew word translated "Leviathan" in this verse comes from *livyathan*, which means "leviathan, sea monster, dragon; a large aquatic animal; perhaps the extinct dinosaur, plesiosaurus," according to Strong's concordance.[1] It goes on to explain, "Some think this to be a crocodile but from the description in Job 41:1–34 this is patently absurd. It appears to be a large fire breathing animal of some sort. Just as the bomardier beetle has an explosion producing mechanism, so the great sea dragon may have an explosive producing mechanism to enable it to be a real fire breathing dragon."[2]

That's pretty intense! So how can we say this is a spirit if it's a fire-breathing dragon? We base this interpretation on hermeneutics' fifth law, the law of double reference, which "is the principle of associating similar or related ideas which are usually separated from one another by long period of times, and which are blended into a single picture like the blending of pictures by a stereopticon."[3]

There are many examples of this in Scripture. Perhaps the best known is in the Book of Daniel where the prince of Persia and the king of Persia are mentioned (Dan. 10:13). The prince of Persia was a principality. The king of Persia was a human being. Likewise, Leviathan was a real beast, but there is a spirit that carries its supernatural, demonic characteristics.

In Near Eastern religions, Leviathan represents the forces of chaos. That is perhaps the first sign of a Leviathan spirit's operation. If chaos is marking your life or your church— ongoing chaos and drama that cannot be calmed or settled—a Leviathan spirit likely is at work. But there were probably other signs that went unnoticed before full-blown chaos erupted. You may not have connected the dots between what appeared as a work of the flesh and Leviathan. Let's drill down into the characteristics of this destructive spirit.

LEVIATHAN IS A GOSSIPING DIVIDER

Gossip is one of the first manifestations of a Leviathan spirit. Again, Job 41:1 says, "Can you draw out Leviathan with a hook or snare his tongue with a line which you let down?" Gossip is a sin in itself, but Leviathan influences people to pile sin upon sin because the intent of its gossip is to breed strife and division.

James 3:6 reveals, "The tongue is a fire, a world of evil. The tongue is among the parts of the body, defiling the whole body, and setting the course of nature on fire, and it is set on fire by hell." And James 3:16 teaches us, "For where there is envying and strife, there is confusion and every evil work." During my encounter with the Leviathan spirit operating through my spiritual brother, gossip and strife immediately manifested over my inability to call him back within an hour—and it was all downhill from there.

Moving on to verses 3 and 4 of Job 41, we read: "Will he make many supplications to you? Will he speak soft words to you? Will he make a covenant with you? Will you take him for a servant forever?" Leviathan is a covenant-breaking spirit. Isaiah 27:1 calls Leviathan "the fleeing spirit." That word "fleeing" is from the Hebrew *bariyach*, which means "fugitive." [4] A fugitive is one who runs away to avoid being caught. Leviathan wants the person to flee before he can get delivered.

When this spirit rages, those who come under its influence will break covenant with you without a second thought and with no apology. That's what happened with my spiritual brother. Within weeks he resigned the ministry and moved out of the state. One minute he was pledging to run anywhere the Lord leads—and really meant it—and the next minute he was in Leviathan's covenant-breaking grip. Of course, it doesn't happen that fast, but it sure seems like it.

Next we see the impact of the words of a person under the influence of a Leviathan spirit—or the imaginations Leviathan releases against the mind. These are words that will burn, wound, and otherwise seek to harm. Leviathan's fiery darts strike the heart. "His sneezing flashes forth light, and his eyes are like the eyelids of the morning. Out of his mouth go burning lights, and sparks of fire leap out. Out of his nostrils goes smoke as out of a seething pot or cauldron. His breath kindles coals, and a flame goes out of his mouth" (Job 41:18–21).

Leviathan also twists situations and words. People under this spirit's influence see things much differently from reality. They hear words you did not say or take the words you do say to mean something you never intended. It's no wonder Isaiah 27:1 calls Leviathan "the twisted serpent."

LEVIATHAN'S OPPRESSIVE TACTICS

Leviathan is nothing to play with, and you can't put this spirit on a leash or appease it with compromise. Consider the wisdom in Job 41:5–7: "Will you play with him as with a bird? Or will you put him on a leash for your maidens? Will your companions make a banquet of him? Will they divide him among the merchants? Can you fill his skin with harpoons or his head with fishing spears?"

This passage uses harpoons and fishing spears as metaphors for spiritual weapons, indicating that Leviathan won't bow to common warfare tactics. You can't just bind this and move on—it is a principality and it's hard to penetrate. When it manifests in a person's thinking, you can't win him over easily. He is convinced his view is right and yours is wrong. People can repent of giving their minds over to Leviathan's twisted attack, but freedom requires the Lord's intervention.

This spirit is intimidating and bullies most people from contending with it. Again we see in Job: "Lay your hand on him; remember the battle—you will do it no more. Notice, any hope of overcoming him is in vain; shall not one be overwhelmed at the sight of him? No one is so fierce that he dares to stir him up" (Job 41:8–10). Verses 13–14 continue this terrible theme: "Who can remove his outer garment? Or who can approach him with a double bridle? Who can open the jaws of his face? His teeth are terrible all around."

Verses 24–29 continue the intimidation: "His heart is as firm as a stone, yes, as hard as a piece of the lower millstone. When he raises up himself even the gods are afraid; because of his crashings they are beside themselves. The sword that reaches him cannot avail, nor does the spear, the arrow, or the javelin. He counts iron as straw, and brass as rotten wood. The arrow cannot make him flee; slingstones are turned into stubble by him. Arrows are counted as straw; he laughs at the shaking of a spear."

That's a frightening description of this principality. Consider the words of Job in chapter 3. We find Job cursing the day of his birth, and he says in verse 8, "Let them curse it who curse any day, those who are prepared to rouse Leviathan."

Of course, God is able to stand against Leviathan, and He reminds Job of that reality: "Who then is able to stand before Me? Who has preceded Me that I should repay him? Everything under heaven is Mine" (Job 41:10–11). In Psalm 74:14 the psalmist declares, "You crushed the heads of Leviathan in pieces." And with regard to the deliverance of Israel in the end times, the Bible says, "In that day the Lord with His fierce and great and strong sword shall punish Leviathan the fleeing serpent, even Leviathan the twisted serpent; and He shall slay the dragon that is in the sea" (Isa. 27:1).

Leviathan is an oppressing spirit, and if you've come under its bonds you will usually need help to break free from its intimidating influence. Resist it at its onset before it puts a hook in your nose and uses your tongue to gossip and bring division. Again, those under Leviathan's influence will not only break covenant with you, they will also flee from you despite God's plan. But know this: even though Leviathan makes people flee, this divisive spirit itself is still operating in your midst.

Of Leviathan the Bible says, "He makes the deep to boil like a pot; he makes the sea like a pot of ointment. He leaves a shining wake behind him; one would think the deep had white hair" (Job 41:31–32). This spirit likes to bring issues to a boiling point and keep them stirred up. This is part of its chaotic assignment. Even if it moves out for a season, it will leave a wake—a rippling effect in your life that may not settle before this principality strikes again.

Leviathan also works to bring sorrow into your life: "Strength dwells in his neck, and sorrow dances before him" (Job 41:22, NKJV). Given Leviathan's gossip and covenant-breaking, haughty, divisive, chaotic attacks, it's easy to see how a person would feel grief and sorrow in the wake of an attack. Leviathan's heart is as hard as stone (Job 41:24), and this spirit influences its victims to become hard-hearted toward you and, if there is no intervention, eventually the things of the Spirit.

LEVIATHAN'S ARROGANT ROOTS

Pride opens the door to Leviathan's influence in someone's life. Although we all have a measure of pride, you've probably noticed that some people are especially haughty. Everything has to be their way. They are always right and everyone else is always wrong. Even if they are wrong, they will not admit it. The Bible has plenty to say about pride, but I'll give you a quick summary so you can see just how dangerous it is.

- "The fear of the LORD is to hate evil; pride and arrogance and the evil way and the perverse mouth I hate" (Prov. 8:13).

- "When pride comes, then comes shame" (Prov. 11:2).

- "Everyone who is proud in heart is an abomination to the LORD; be assured, he will not be unpunished" (Prov. 16:5).

- "Do you see a man wise in his own conceit? There is more hope for a fool than for him" (Prov. 26:12).

- "Pride goes before destruction, and a haughty spirit before a fall" (Prov. 16:18).

- "A high look, a proud heart, and the plowing of the wicked are sin" (Prov. 21:4).

- "A man's pride will bring him low" (Prov. 29:23).

I could go on and on. Those are just the proverbs. The Bible warns against pride again and again. I believe pride, especially spiritual pride, opens the door to spirits and blinds people to the reality that they are under the influence of a spirit other than God. The Leviathan spirit in particular will find easy cooperation with someone who has excessive pride.

People who operate in pride have common ground with Leviathan. Job 41:15–17 reads, "His scales are his pride, shut up tightly as with a seal. One is so near to another that no air can come between them. They are joined to each other; they stick together that they cannot be separated." Job 41:34 describes Leviathan this way: "He beholds all high things; he is a king over all the children of pride."

Indeed, spiritual pride is a monstrous problem in the body of Christ. Some have spiritual pride because of their position in a church. Others have spiritual pride because of social media popularity. Still others have spiritual pride in their prayer life. You'll notice that people who operate in spiritual pride are convinced they are more anointed, more discerning, more gifted, more eloquent, more powerful, more revelatory, more important, and generally more spiritual than others. Spiritual pride manifests as self-righteousness, hypercritical attitudes, hypocrisy, scorning correction or guidance, putting on pretenses, and false humility.

Although God hates pride, spiritual pride is especially dangerous. The problem with pride in any form is that those deceived by self-glorification, self-sufficiency, self-admiration, egoism, and self-trust are too proud to consider they may be offending the Lord. You may see people operating in spiritual gifts in public who have deplorable character in private. That doesn't mean God doesn't see the condition of their hearts; rather, it means the gifts and callings of God are without repentance and the Lord is blessing the hungry who came expecting a breakthrough. Pride always leads to a fall, and many times the proud fall into Leviathan's snare.

Ironically, pride can hamper a believer's ability to battle

this principality. Some spiritual warriors take so much pride in their spiritual warfare prowess that the common ground with this haughty spirit hinders their authority. As I said earlier in the book, you can't act like the devil and take authority over the devil at the same time.

Remember, the Bible says we can be "ready to punish all disobedience when your obedience is complete" (2 Cor. 10:6). That doesn't mean you need to be perfect to exercise your authority, but you should repent of any known sin before engaging in the battle. We can't take on Leviathan or any other spirit in our own strength. We need the grace of God. James offers good advice for spiritual warriors:

> But He gives more grace. For this reason it says: "God resists the proud, but gives grace to the humble." Therefore submit yourselves to God. Resist the devil, and he will flee from you. Draw near to God, and He will draw near to you. Cleanse your hands, you sinners, and purify your hearts, you double-minded. Grieve and mourn and weep. Let your laughter be turned to mourning, and your joy to dejection. Humble yourselves in the sight of the Lord, and He will lift you up.
>
> —James 4:6–10

So take a moment now to examine your heart before you pray the following prayer.

A PRAYER TO LOOSE YOU FROM LEVIATHAN'S LIES

There is some debate in the body of Christ as to whether you can combat Leviathan in the way you would other demons.

Rather than debate both sides here, I've decided to offer a prayer that works either way:

> *Father, I thank You that Your Word is truth. Your Word is purified seven times. Your Word is alive and sharper than any two-edged sword. The truth in Your Word sets me free from Leviathan's twisted lies. I ask You to forgive me for believing Leviathan's lies and help me to discern this twisting dragon's tall tales.*
>
> *Father, cut off the head of this dreadful dragon. Break this principality into pieces for Your name's sake. Crush this crooked criminal spirit with Your strong sword. Slay this water spirit with Your Word. I come against the deceptions this sea spirit has introduced into my mind. I release the sword of the Lord against it. Rip off its scales, Lord. Break its back. Break its teeth. Rebuke it in its pride. Bring this haughty devil low.*
>
> *I break loose from Leviathan's oppression. I shake and break free from the assaults against my mind, my will, my emotions, and my body. I command a drought to come into Leviathan's waters. Dry up its resting place. O God, smite it with Your mighty hand and deliver me from this demonic onslaught in the name of Jesus. Amen.*

CHAPTER 4

PYTHON'S PERILOUS SQUEEZE

I'VE JOKED THAT I lived in a pressure cooker, but it wasn't deadline stress at *Charisma* magazine that was overwhelming my soul—it was a potent principality attacking my physical person. I didn't *feel* like praying. I didn't *feel* like worshipping. And, honestly, I didn't *feel* like that would ever change. I didn't immediately discern it, but the python spirit had wrapped itself around me and was squeezing the want-to out of me.

The only thing I *felt* like doing was curling up in a ball with my favorite blanket and escaping the world. Of course, that's exactly what the python spirit—or any spirit for that matter—wants us to do in the heat of the battle. I urge you to understand this principle: if you lay down your mighty weapons in the midst of the onslaught, the enemy will not agree to a truce. If you meditate on the emotions and imaginations hitting your mind, you're allowing the enemy to bring destruction in your life. You must determine in your heart now to keep your armor on at all times.

I learned that the hard way. The python spirit is active in many nations of the world, but this principality is stronger in some territories than in others and, sadly, it has a chokehold on my region. No one warned me. No one taught me.

I discovered this diabolical demon after I personally encountered its estrapade—its attempt to throw me from my place.[1] Revelation arose regarding this villainous spiritual vermin only after it spiraled around me with a vengeance—and I had to break free from its death grip.

The python spirit is in the crosshairs of many spiritual warriors, and practical revelation about how this demon operates has surfaced in recent years. Still, there are many who aren't aware of this enemy's devices. Symptoms of a python attack may include weariness, a loss of passion to worship and pray, or feeling pressured, overwhelmed, helpless, and even hopeless. The severity of those symptoms depends on how long this irreligious reptile has been coiling itself around you—and how much pressure it has applied to your soul.

"A python is after one thing: *breath*. It slowly coils itself around its victim and begins to squeeze the life out, little by little; as its grip gets tighter and tighter, it chokes and suffocates its prey until all the air is expunged from the prey's lungs,"[2] Jentezen Franklin wrote in his book *The Spirit of Python*. "Do you feel as if you are losing your passion for the Lord, for the Word, for prayer, and for praise? Don't brush it off as a spiritual slump. Understand that this is the python tactic of the enemy. Are you facing battle after battle, problem after problem, in your home, your marriage, your family, your finances, or your job? Begin to recognize this as the work of the python."[3]

WHAT IS THE PYTHON SPIRIT?

One of the only named spirits in the Bible, the python spirit is a coiling spirit that works to squeeze out the breath of life (the Holy Spirit) and cut off your lifeline to God (prayer). To accomplish its deadly agenda, this spirit will remind you of wounds from your past, surround you with ungodly influences that tempt you to compromise the Word of God, or just barrage you with circumstances that knock the wind out of you.

The python principality is seen in Acts 16:16 when Paul encounters a girl possessed with a spirit of divination. The word *divination* in this verse comes from the Greek word *pythōn*, which translates in English as "python."[4] Vine's expository dictionary explains that according to Greek mythology, the Pythian serpent guarded the oracle of Delphi until Apollo slew it and then took on the name Pythian. The word was later applied to diviners or soothsayers, who were seen as inspired by Apollo.[5]

We also see the python rising in the Old Testament. The Darby translation, which was first published in 1890 by an Anglo-Irish Bible teacher to offer a then-modern translation for the average person,[6] pulls out what we may not otherwise have seen. In various scriptures the python is connected to divination, as we can see clearly in the Darby Translation:

> And if there be a man or a woman in whom is a spirit of Python or of divination, they shall certainly be put to death: they shall stone them with stones; their blood is upon them.
> —Leviticus 20:27, Darby

> There shall not be found among you he that maketh his son or his daughter to pass through the fire, that useth divination, that useth auguries, or an enchanter, or a sorcerer, or a charmer, or one that inquireth of

a spirit of Python, or a soothsayer, or one that consulteth the dead.

—Deuteronomy 18:10–11, Darby

Then said Saul to his servants, Seek me a woman that has a spirit of Python, that I may go to her and inquire of her. And his servants said to him, Behold, there is a woman who has a spirit of Python at En-dor. And Saul disguised himself, and put on other garments, and he went, and two men with him, and they came to the woman by night; and he said, I pray thee, divine to me by the spirit of Python, and bring me [him] up whom I shall name to thee.

—1 Samuel 28:7–8, Darby

And Saul died for his unfaithfulness which he committed against Jehovah, because of the word of Jehovah which he kept not, and also for having inquired of the spirit of Python, asking counsel of it.

—1 Chronicles 10:13, Darby

PYTHON'S NATURAL PARALLELS

My territory, South Florida, is home to the Everglades National Park, which is overrun by pythons—and they are moving north. Media are describing it as an invasion.[7] I believe this is a reflection of what is going on in the spirit realm. We can glean from how the python spirit operates by looking at how these nonvenomous snakes, which are known as Old World snakes because they are not native to North or South America, work in the natural.

The python family of snakes are some of the largest in the world, growing over thirty feet long, according to LiveScience.com. They often camouflage themselves based on their environment, and some seek out cold-blooded prey.[8] Spiritually speaking, these spirits blend into their environment and choose not to be seen until they find opportunity to strike, and their first target is often those who are lukewarm or cold toward God. That is why it's important to be discerning and stay on fire for God! It's harder to overtake on-fire believers because they will discern the attack and fight back!

Pythons have sharp, curved teeth that lean backward. They are patient and move slowly until they suddenly ambush their target. Large pythons can eat monkeys, pigs, antelopes, and wallabies. The San Diego Zoo reported that a rock python consumed a small leopard. Pythons have even attacked humans in the natural realm.[9]

The spirit of python attacks humans with a similar slow and patient strategy that waits for the right moment to strike suddenly with a bite—but it's not the bite that kills; it's the pressure. Once thought to kill by crushing, LiveScience reports that pythons actually kill by either suffocating their victims or possibly by cutting off blood from the brain. Once its prey is dead, the python opens its jaws and swallows its victim head first.[10] Thank God we have the blood of Jesus and the serpent is under our feet! But victory over this spirit requires discernment.

PYTHON ATTACKS YOUR PRAYER LIFE

The python spirit can attack anyone. You don't have to be in sin to find python trying to slide under your door. Paul was a man of prayer. The Bible says he spoke in tongues more than anybody else in the Corinthian church (1 Cor. 14:18)—and probably more than anybody else in the early church.

Despite Paul's relationship with Christ and strong prayer

life, he still had to wrestle against principalities, powers, rulers of the darkness of this age, and spiritual hosts of wickedness in the heavenly places (Eph. 6:12). Paul had to wrestle against python—and so may we. Let's look at Paul's encounter with the python spirit.

> On one occasion, as we went to the place of prayer, a servant girl possessed with a spirit of divination met us, who brought her masters much profit by fortune-telling. She followed Paul and us, shouting, "These men are servants of the Most High God, who proclaim to us the way of salvation."...And it came out at that moment.
>
> —ACTS 16:16–18

The python spirit had a stronghold in Philippi. When the man of prayer started heading for the house of prayer, this spirit launched its first attack against him—a distraction followed by a full-blown trial that aimed to take him out of his purpose. Python knows it has no authority in a city that prays in the presence of God, so it works to distract people from praying so they can't fulfill their purpose.

Python would rather watch you lick your wounds than pray to a healing God. Python would rather hear you complain or gossip than take your problems to a miracle-working God. Python would rather distract you with attacks, trials, and persecutions than see you press into a gracious God for deliverance. Again, python's ultimate goal is to put you in bondage and thwart your purpose. You may be going through the motions but feel dead on the inside because python has squeezed the life out of you.

LOOSING YOURSELF FROM PYTHON'S GRIP

When you rise up in your Christ-given authority against python, the battle ensues. Paul cast the demon out of the girl, which meant her masters could no longer profit from her false prophecies. "When her masters saw that the hope of their profits was gone, they seized Paul and Silas, and dragged them into the marketplace to the rulers" (Acts 16:19). From there Paul and Silas were falsely accused, had their clothes torn off, were beaten with rods, and were thrown into prison with stocks on their feet.

Paul and Silas were in physical pain. They had been publicly humiliated. They were slandered and maligned. And they were in the grip of the python spirit. At this point they had several options: They could lie there and lick their wounds. They could complain to one another about their situation. They could meditate on the persecution and decide to abandon their purpose in exchange for being set free. But they didn't do any of that. Thank God, they left us a model for how to break free from the python spirit.

> At midnight Paul and Silas were praying and singing hymns to God, and the prisoners were listening to them. Suddenly there was a great earthquake, so that the foundations of the prison were shaken. And immediately all the doors were opened and everyone's shackles were loosened.
>
> —Acts 16:25–26

Prayer and praise are what python is trying to stop, but prayer and praise will set you free.

In spiritual warfare circles we talk a lot about the armor of God. Some of us even symbolically get dressed in our armor every day. We've memorized Ephesians 6:10–17, but a freedom key is in verse 18: *"Praying always* with *all prayer* and supplication in the Spirit, being watchful to this end with all perseverance and supplication for all the saints" (NKJV, emphasis added).

That's right, wearing heavy battle armor is not enough without prayer—and the right kind of prayer. Remember, Paul was on his way to the house of prayer when python attacked. Python doesn't want you praying in the presence of God because when you are engaging in Spirit-led prayer, you're doing damage to the kingdom of darkness. The enemy knows that your authority in prayer in Christ's name is what sets you free from his oppression—and it's what sets those around you free.

Scripture makes it clear. Paul and Silas were praying and worshipping. The prisoners heard them and saw a mighty miracle. God sent an earthquake that shook the prison, and the doors flung wide open. The Bible says "everyone's chains were loosed." I believe all the prisoners got a taste of God's miracle-working power that day, and Paul's prayer and worship planted gospel seeds in their souls. Your breakthrough is a testimony to someone else in chains if you'll share it. What happened after Paul and Silas prayed supports that theory:

> When the jailer awoke and saw the prison doors open, he drew his sword and would have killed himself, supposing that the prisoners had escaped. But Paul shouted, "Do not harm yourself, for we are all here." He called for lights and rushed in, trembling, and fell down before Paul and Silas. He then led them out and asked, "Sirs, what must I do to be saved?" They said, "Believe in the Lord Jesus Christ, and you and your household will be saved." And they spoke the

word of the Lord to him and to all who were in his household. In that hour of the night he took them and washed their wounds. And immediately he and his entire household were baptized. Then he brought them up to his house and set food before them. And he rejoiced with his entire household believing in God.

—ACTS 16:27–34

Paul's prayer and worship in the midst of a python attack also paved the way for the Lord to vindicate him. When the magistrates called for the jailer to release Paul and Silas, the prison guard told them to go in peace. But Paul pulled his Roman card and demanded his accusers come and bring them out in public. That's what you call God preparing a table for you in the presence of your enemies (Ps. 23:5).

ROOTING PYTHON OUT OF A CITY

Noteworthy is the fact that all this happened in the city of Thyatira. This is where we find that woman Jezebel, who calls herself a prophetess in Revelation 2:20. Jezebel operates in witchcraft, or divination. Put another way, the spirits of Jezebel and python often work together against a target. Jezebel is a spirit of seduction that is successfully tempting many prophetic people to operate in divination.

Keep in mind that the prayers and praise of Paul and Silas set the captives free, but the spirit of python was still reigning over the city when they left on the next leg of their mission. The python spirit can reign in a life or a region where people are ignorant of the devil's devices. (See 2 Corinthians 2:11.)

We need revelation from the Holy Spirit about what is operating in our lives and in our territories in order to ultimately root it out and set up a guard against its reentry by our authority in Christ. Now here's the rub: although many have come to understand python's life-squeezing, breath-stealing tactics, we too often fail to engage in Spirit-led prayer that would render this principality powerless.

This python spirit is a major influence in Florida, where we have more houses of prayer per capita than almost any other state at the time of this writing. Python is so spiritually active in our state that it has manifested with an overrun of natural pythons in the Everglades. Experts point to as many as 100,000 Burmese pythons in the Florida Everglades that are reproducing rapidly. This snake is driving down populations of opossums, bobcats, and raccoons and even swallows deer and alligators whole.[11]

Although reciting rote prayers from a book may push back darkness for a moment, ultimately that spiritual warfare strategy isn't going to deliver you—and keep you free—from python's grip. Freedom from python demands fervent intercession. It starts with repentance and works its way into travailing prayer by the leading of the Spirit of God (Rom. 8:26–27).

What do we do, practically speaking? We need to pray to the righteous Lord who "has cut in pieces the cords of the wicked" (Ps. 129:4, NKJV)—the cords python has coiled around us. We need to repent for our sins—and the sins of our cities—that have allowed python a stronghold so God can surround us with songs of deliverance in His presence (Ps. 32:7). We have authority in Christ to cut in pieces this coiling spirit, but again it often takes travailing prayer with the Spirit of God to free the body from the head of the snake in a region.

A POWERFUL PRAYER AGAINST
THE PYTHON PRINCIPALITY

We are not powerless over the python spirit. Use the following as a prayer starter to break the power of this spirit over your life and region:

Father, I come to You in the name of Jesus and in His authority. I take authority over the python spirit operating in any and every area of my life, including my mind, will, and emotions; my physical body; my relationships; and my finances. Yes, I come against every manifestation of python's coiling grip in my life.

I stand against this serpentine devil that is working to constrict the flow of Your light and life in my heart. I break the powers of this spiritual wickedness that is working to hinder my prayer life, my praise, and my worship. I reject spiritual apathy, feeling overwhelmed, hopelessness, and weariness. I sever its coils and break the power of its lies.

I cancel python's assignment against me and my city. I root out all of the eggs python has laid in my life and territory. I command its twisting and turning ways to cease and desist. I refuse to fear python spirits. Like the devil himself, this spirit is under my feet. Strengthen me for battle. Crush the head of the snake. I destroy its den. I tread upon it, for it cannot harm me.

I decree and declare that I am delivered and set free from the python's grip. I decree and declare that my prayer life will carry more fire, more wind, and more anointing. I decree and declare that my praise will release more power and my worship is my warfare. I thank You, Lord, for fighting for, through, and with me, in the name of Jesus. Amen.

PART TWO

POWERS THAT PRESS
AGAINST THE SAINTS

CHAPTER 5

RELIGION'S UNRIGHTEOUS RULES

As a woman in ministry, I've stood toe-to-toe against the spirit of religion many times. People—male and female—have told me I can't preach, pray, or prophesy. Others concede I can stand behind a pulpit so long as I don a big hat and don't wear makeup or earrings. I've been vilified, defamed, libeled, smeared, disparaged, maligned, slighted, and otherwise persecuted in the name of Jesus. I take comfort in knowing Jesus experienced all this in the name of the Father.

Religion is a murdering spirit. People in bondage to religious spirits murdered Jesus, Stephen, and the apostles—and they want to murder you. They may not crucify you, stone you, or behead you in the natural, but these self-righteous serial killers have you on a spiritual hit list. They will assassinate your character and massacre your reputation if you refuse to submit to their ridiculous, irreligious rules.

The spirit of religion is a murderous demon that seeks to heap condemnation on the saints. It sets up rules that no one can keep perfectly and works to strip us of our true identity as the righteousness of God in Christ Jesus. Religious spirits seek to weigh us down either with guilt and condemnation or, on the other end of the spectrum, pride.

When we do what we're called to do—whether that's preach, pray, prophesy, or tackle some other God-given assignment—it's bound to make the enemy angry. And when the spirit of religion meets with the spirit of anger, it gets ugly in a hurry.

I believe hypocrisy is the heartbeat of the religious spirit. A person may walk in obedience to the Lord—walking in love with his brothers and sisters in Christ—but then he'll hit a point where he thinks something just isn't "God." Or he'll make decisions based on what certain church leaders think he should do. Only when he crosses that line and chooses to follow man-made rules and rituals instead of the Word of God will he see the religious spirit manifest in all its wickedness.

The woman caught in the act of adultery is a good example. In John 8 the scribes and Pharisees brought Jesus a woman caught in sin—in the very act of adultery. They wanted to see her stoned and asked Jesus what He had to say about it. But you'll notice they didn't drag the man alongside her to be punished. Hypocrisy!

Of course, that is not the only way religion manifests. The apostle Peter wasn't likely to stone anyone for adultery. He understood the work of the Cross—but only up to a point. Peter and Barnabas were enjoying eating with the Gentile converts in Antioch until the Jewish brethren came to visit from Jerusalem. Then he distanced himself from them. Paul rebuked him for his hypocrisy (Gal. 2:11–21). It was a religious spirit at work.

WHAT JESUS SAID ABOUT
RELIGIOUS SPIRITS

Jesus pronounced woe nineteen times in the New Testament (if you take out the repeated incidents in the Gospels). He pronounced woe to Chorazin and Bethsaida for not repenting after they had seen the mighty miracles He worked (Matt. 11:20–22). He pronounced woe to the world because of temptations and to the man by whom temptation comes (Matt. 18:6–8). He pronounced woe to those who are pregnant or nursing babies during the Great Tribulation (Matt. 24:15–20). And He pronounced woe to the one who betrays the Son of Man (Mark 14:21).

Most of the woes, however, were pronounced on the scribes and Pharisees—many of whom were under the influence of a religious spirit. So what exactly, then, is a woe? At its root a woe is "a primary exclamation of grief," according to Strong's concordance.[1] Merriam-Webster's dictionary also defines *woe* as a word "used to express grief, regret, or distress."[2] That's appropriate, because people operating in a religious spirit will grieve you and stress you out!

Let's take a look at what these religious operatives did to grieve the Spirit of God within Jesus and why He pronounced woes. In His Matthew 23 discourse, which comes before His warnings about the end times, Jesus starts out by telling His listeners not to act like the scribes and Pharisees because "they speak, but do nothing" (v. 3). I like the punch packed in *The Message* Bible's translation of the passage:

> Instead of giving you God's Law as food and drink by which you can banquet on God, they package it in bundles of rules, loading you down like pack animals. They seem to take pleasure in watching you stagger

under these loads, and wouldn't think of lifting a finger to help. Their lives are perpetual fashion shows, embroidered prayer shawls one day and flowery prayers the next. They love to sit at the head table at church dinners, basking in the most prominent positions, preening in the radiance of public flattery, receiving honorary degrees, and getting called "Doctor" and "Reverend."

—MATTHEW 23:4–7

People operating in a religious spirit load you up with rules like pack animals. They love to watch you struggle and strain to keep a law they aren't keeping themselves. Practically speaking, they chide you for not being at the prayer meeting even though they didn't show up themselves. They have a double-standard. Some of them wear fancy clothes and judge you because you don't do the same. They take front-row seats without being asked to do so and glory in the praise of men. Oh, and the titles. They love the titles! A woman on Facebook sent me a friend request. Her given name was prefaced by "Exalted Prophetess." I decided I wasn't worthy to tie her shoelaces and deleted the request. I'm not against titles, but how many do you need? I've seen everything from Bishop, Doctor, and Reverend to Chief Apostle and Master Prophet of the Most High.

Jesus continues in Matthew 23:8–12:

> Don't let people do that to you, put you on a pedestal like that. You all have a single Teacher, and you are all classmates. Don't set people up as experts over your life, letting them tell you what to do. Save that authority for God; let him tell you what to do. No one else should carry the title of "Father"; you have only one Father, and he's in heaven. And don't let people

maneuver you into taking charge of them. There is only one Life-Leader for you and them—Christ. Do you want to stand out? Then step down. Be a servant. If you puff yourself up, you'll get the wind knocked out of you. But if you're content to simply be yourself, your life will count for plenty.

—The Message

Here Jesus is warning His followers not to operate in a religious spirit but to move in the opposite spirit of what the leadership was modeling at that time. Many in the church today are just propagating a religious paradigm their grannies, mamas, aunties, and others who had influence over their lives passed down the line. The religious showboating may get people up on their feet and pull money out of sincere people's pockets, but it's not the anointing of God and it won't change lives. Remember, the spirit of religion condemns you for not living up to rules that are unreasonable.

PRONOUNCE WOE ON THE SPIRIT, NOT THE PERSON

Jesus pronounced eight woes on the scribes and Pharisees—and He gave good reasons for them. Again, a woe is an exclamation of grief or distress. It denotes anguish, misery, affliction, gloom, sorrow, wretchedness, pain, regret, and rue. We can learn plenty from the woes Jesus pronounced in Matthew 23. Let's begin with verse 15:

> Woe to you, scribes and Pharisees, hypocrites! You travel sea and land to make one proselyte, and when he becomes one, you make him twice as much a son of hell as yourselves.

From this we learn that those under the religious spirit's reign are hypocrites. Merriam-Webster's dictionary defines a hypocrite as "a person who puts on a false appearance of virtue or religion."[3] The reason so many people think Christians are hypocrites is because they haven't met an on-fire believer. They've met only the scribes and Pharisees. Those operating in a religious spirit want to disciple you and turn your heart from the life-giving Spirit of God to the letter of the law, which kills your hunger for the Holy One of Israel (2 Cor. 3:6).

> Woe to you, blind guides, who say, "If anyone swears by the temple, it is nothing. But if anyone swears by the gold of the temple, he is obligated." You blind fools! Which is greater, the gold or the temple that sanctifies the gold? And you say, "If anyone swears by the altar, it is nothing. But if anyone swears by the gift on it, he is obligated." You blind fools! Which is greater, the gift or the altar that sanctifies the gift? Therefore he who swears by the altar, swears by it and by all things on it. But he who swears by the temple, swears by it and by Him who dwells in it. And he who swears by heaven, swears by the throne of God and by Him who sits on it.
>
> —MATTHEW 23:16–22

People functioning out of a religious mind-set are "blind guides." Jesus wasn't talking about people wearing dark glasses and walking with canes. He was talking about the "mentally blind," which is one definition for the Greek word *typhlos* that is translated "blind" in verse 16.[4] The word translated "guide" in verse 16 is from the Greek *hodēgos*, which in this context means "a teacher of the ignorant and inexperienced."[5] Religious spirits are mentally blind to the power of the gospel and teach others in the same way. Paul told Timothy that in the last days people would arise who have a form of godliness but deny its power, and he told his spiritual son to stay away from them (2 Tim. 3:5)! Jesus also called these religious leaders "fools," which comes from the Greek word *mōros* that means "foolish, impious, godless." [6] What an indictment!

> Woe to you, scribes and Pharisees, hypocrites! You tithe mint and dill and cumin, but have neglected the weightier matters of the law: justice and mercy and faith. These you ought to have done without leaving the others undone. You blind guides who strain out a gnat and swallow a camel!
>
> —MATTHEW 23:23–24

Religious hypocrites don't love you. They have no mercy on you when you fail to live up to their unreasonable expectations. And they are more interested in judgment than justice.

> Woe to you, scribes and Pharisees, hypocrites! You cleanse the outside of the cup and dish, but inside they are full of extortion and greed. You blind Pharisee, first cleanse the inside of the cup and dish, that the outside of them may also be clean.
>
> —MATTHEW 23:25–26

The word translated "extortion" in verse 25 comes from the Greek word *harpagē*, meaning "the act of plundering, robbery." [7] People operating in a religious spirit will take every penny you have in the name of Jesus to build their own irreverent kingdom. Don't sow into a religious spirit's offering, because you won't reap anything righteous.

Religious spirits are more interested in making their name famous than making Christ's name famous.

> Woe to you, scribes and Pharisees, hypocrites! You are like whitewashed tombs, which indeed appear beautiful outwardly, but inside are full of dead men's bones and of all uncleanness. So you also outwardly appear righteous to men, but inside you are full of hypocrisy and iniquity.
>
> —Matthew 23:27–28

Most of Christ's words in verses 27 and 28 speak for themselves, but it's noteworthy to point out the "iniquity," which comes from the Greek word *anomia*. It means "the condition of without law," either because of ignorance to it or violating it, and "contempt and violation of law, iniquity, wickedness."[8] If the Pharisees loved the law, they would love the people, but their actions demonstrate hatred instead. The religious spirit is a hateful spirit.

> Woe to you, scribes and Pharisees, hypocrites! You build the tombs of the prophets, and adorn the memorials of the righteous, and say, "If we lived in the days of our fathers, we would not have partaken with them in shedding the blood of the prophets." Therefore you are witnesses against yourselves that you are sons of those who murdered the prophets. Fill up, then, the measure of your fathers' guilt.
>
> —Matthew 23:29–32

Like the spirit of Jezebel, the religious spirit wants to cut off the prophetic voice. Again, it's a murdering spirit that does not want to hear what the Lord is saying. It wants to set rules over and beyond what Jesus requires. Although the

Ten Commandments in Exodus are still legitimate, Jesus summed them all up in John 13:34–35: "A new commandment I give to you, that you love one another, even as I have loved you, that you also love one another. By this all men will know that you are My disciples, if you have love for one another."

Jesus pronounced woe on the scribes and Pharisees. In Matthew 23:33 He calls them hopeless, reptilian snakes (THE MESSAGE), which the Amplified Bible, Classic Edition translates as a "spawn of vipers." Jesus asked them, "How can you escape the judgment of hell?" The religious spirit will not escape hell, but we should pray for those who are under its influence. We should pray that they will escape its bondage. We should pray that they will repent before the woe falls on them.

COMBATING RELIGION'S INTIMIDATION TACTICS

The enemy often stirs up modern-day Pharisees to intimidate, manipulate, and malign God's people. It grieves the Holy Spirit, but the enemy is an expert at convincing Christians to threaten and even try to publicly shame those who don't agree with them and refuse to bow to their ungodly will.

It's called religious witchcraft, which Paul lists as a work of the flesh, alongside "adultery, sexual immorality, impurity, lewdness, idolatry, sorcery, hatred, strife, jealousy, rage, selfishness, dissensions, heresies, envy, murders, drunkenness, carousing, and the like" (Gal. 5:19–21). In case you are wondering how serious religious witchcraft really is, Paul went on to say that those who practice it would not inherit the kingdom of God.

Religious witchcraft is not new. We see it manifesting

in the early days of the church against Holy Spirit–led believers. A prime example is found in Acts 4. The religious rulers arrested Peter and John for preaching the resurrection of Jesus. The Sanhedrin wanted to know by what name or power they healed the man at the Gate Beautiful. Empowered by the Holy Ghost, Peter essentially preached the gospel to them (vv. 1–12).

That is when the intimidation, manipulation, and maligning began. First, the religious rulers "commanded them not to speak or teach at all in the name of Jesus" (v. 18). That didn't sit too well with Peter, who immediately told them he must obey God in the matter. In other words, Peter told them he wouldn't stop doing what God called him to do or change the way he was doing it to please any man.

What did the religious leaders do? They threatened him and John and let them go—but not for long. In Acts 5 we see persevering Peter still doing what God called him to do. The religious leaders started boiling over with anger. The Bible says the religious leaders "were filled with indignation, and laid their hands on the apostles and put them in the common prison" (vv. 17–18, NKJV). And when Peter wouldn't stop doing what he was called to do despite the punishment, "they were furious and plotted to kill them" (v. 33, NKJV). Here we see the murderous intent of the religious spirit.

When the religious spirit met with the spirit of anger, the apostles were beaten and once again told not to speak in the name of Jesus (v. 40). The religious leaders shamed the apostles, but the apostles didn't stop doing what they were called to do (vv. 41–42). These are not isolated incidents. Scripture also reveals religious intimidators stoned both Stephen (Acts 7:59) and Paul (Acts 14:19).

NEVERTHELESS, DON'T BOW TO RELIGION

Thankfully, that didn't stop these believers from staying the course. The apostles picked up their crosses and followed Jesus. They crucified their flesh. They walked in a manner worthy of the Lord. The religious leaders, by contrast, allowed the enemy to work through their flesh to manipulate, intimidate, and malign the apostles—or at least try their level best to do so. The apostles didn't care what sorts of threats the religious leaders or anyone else were making against them. The only one they would bow to was Jesus.

Clearly, a Spirit-led Christian won't practice fulfilling the lust of the flesh (Gal. 5:16). But a devil-led Christian will release all sorts of intimidating threats against you in order to scare you into submission to the enemy's will. I've experienced this far too often in Christendom through leaders and laymen alike. I have learned to discern the subtlest form of manipulation before it manifests as a full-blown threat and to prepare my heart for the onslaught. I've learned to keep my mouth shut, my head down, and my heart tender toward the Lord. And I'm still learning.

So when you discern religious witchcraft—which often manifests as intimidation, manipulation, and maligning—don't try to defend yourself. Let the Lord vindicate you. Don't stop doing what God told you to do. Keep pressing into your kingdom assignment with confidence that God has your back—because He does. And try praying this prayer. It always helps me: "Now, Lord, look on their threats and grant that Your servants may speak Your word with great boldness, by stretching out Your hand to heal and that signs and wonders may be performed in the name of Your holy Son Jesus" (Acts 4:29–30).

A PRAYER TO ROUT RELIGIOUS DEMONS

Are you ready to rout the demonic religious bullies plaguing your life? This prayer will send them packing—but remember it's not a once-and-for-all battle:

Father, thank You for sending Your Son, Jesus, to the cross to pay the price for my sins so I could have a relationship with You. I repent of any religious thinking that has caused me to see You wrongly, and I renounce all religious mind-sets. Please help me to renew my mind. I renounce all legalism, traditionalism, dead works, and intellectualism I have embraced knowingly or unknowingly.

Lord, forgive me of man-pleasing, compromising Your Word at any level, or having hypocrisy in my life. I repent of self-righteousness, rebellion, and pride. I reject even the inkling of a murderous spirit that would seek to operate through my thought life or my mouth. Shine Your light of truth on my heart and remove any religious deception in which I walk. Teach me Your true ways and show me Your true paths. Let the words of my mouth and the meditation of my heart be pleasing in Your sight.

Now, in the name of Jesus, I break the power of religious spirits operating against me. I bind all religious witchcraft released at my mind. I command the religious spirit to cease and desist its operations to murder my reputation, influence my mind, or lead me away from Your truth. I combat the religious spirit's persecution in my life and ask You to deliver those who are enslaved to this wicked mind-set. I decree and declare that where the Spirit of the

Lord is there is liberty. I will bow to Your Spirit alone, and I will not follow any spirit that leads me once again into the bondage from which You've delivered me. Amen.

CHAPTER 6

WITCHCRAFT'S WICKED POWER

W HEN I WAS a kid, some of my favorite shows were *The Munsters*, *I Dream of Jeannie*, *The Addams Family*, and, of course, *Bewitched*. All of those shows had one thing in common: there was an element of the supernatural, specifically witchcraft. With so much witchcraft in mainstream entertainment—from *Harry Potter* to *Sabrina the Teenage Witch* to *Game of Thrones* and beyond—it's easy to misunderstand spiritual witchcraft.

It's not likely that you are going to run into a boy wizard or a teenage witch. The Bible talks about witchcraft in a different sense. In Ephesians 6:12 witchcraft is listed as a power in the demonic hierarchy—principalities, powers, the rulers of the darkness of this age, and spiritual forces of wickedness in the heavenly places. I believe various principalities, including Jezebel, python, and leviathan, release witchcraft as a power to inflict degrees of suffering on people.

Looking at witchcraft from a biblical perspective, spiritual witchcraft is a power of the enemy that targets your mind and sometimes your body. Spiritual witchcraft taps into the power of death and life that is in our tongues with a goal to manipulate, control, and dominate. When someone guilts, pressures, intimidates, or otherwise plays with your emotions to get you to bow to their will, that is witchcraft at work. When someone curses you with their mouth, that is a form of witchcraft. We know that witchcraft is rebellion against God because His Word forbids it. While witchcraft can come from actual witches or voodoo, most often it comes from principalities, Christians releasing word curses, or your own disobedience. I go much deeper into how witchcraft functions in my book *Satan's Deadly Trio*.

The first instance of witchcraft we see in the Bible is when Saul disobeyed the Lord. The prophet Samuel told him "rebellion is as the sin of witchcraft" (1 Sam. 15:23). Witchcraft in that verse means just that—witchcraft—and it comes from the Hebrew word *qecem* (sometimes *kehsem*). In this context it is associated with Balaam and false prophets.[1] False prophets are one of the sources of witchcraft in the church. One definition of witchcraft is "the use of sorcery or magic; communication with the devil or with a familiar; an irresistible influence or fascination."[2] Many false prophets are tapping into witchcraft via familiar spirits.

The next instance of witchcraft is found concerning Queen Jezebel and her "witchcrafts" (2 Kings 9:22, KJV). In this scripture witchcraft comes from the Hebrew word *kesheph*, which means sorcery and witchcraft.[3] It comes from the root word *kashaph*, which means to whisper, as in whispering a spell.[4] We know that Queen Jezebel sent a messenger to curse Elijah. Her words cast a spell of fear on him that sent the man of God running for his life.

We also see witchcraft in the New Testament in Paul's list of works of the flesh in Galatians 5:20. This Greek word translated "witchcraft" in that verse (*pharmakeia*) has several meanings: "the use or the administering of drugs; poisoning; sorcery, magical arts, often found in connection with idolatry and fostered by it"; and a metaphor for "the deceptions and seductions of idolatry." 5

I believe witchcraft often begins in most Christians as a work of the flesh, but if someone practices this sin, it opens a door for them to operate in a higher realm of spiritual witchcraft and their tongue becomes a spiritual force or weapon in the hands of the enemy. Again, the power of death and life are in the tongue (Prov. 18:21). Anyone can operate in witchcraft—and many Christians do.

YES, THERE IS WITCHCRAFT IN THE CHURCH

Most of us focus on the psychic shops and witchcraft-laced entertainment and cry foul. But there is witchcraft in the church. No, Christians are not reading tarot cards, mixing potions, or casting spells—at least I hope not—but many are practicing witchcraft.

Remember when King Saul was ordered to utterly destroy the Amalekites and everything they had: man, woman, infant and suckling, ox and sheep, camel and ass? Saul found victory in battle against Israel's enemy by the grace of God but failed to obey the voice of God when the dust settled. He spared Agag, the king of the Amalekites, and kept the best of the livestock. (See 1 Samuel 15:1–9.)

Saul proposed that his intention was to sacrifice the animals to the Lord, but there is no excuse for disobedience. Saul was so stubborn that he at first refused to admit his disobedience. He actually justified his actions. Only after Samuel rebuked Saul did the king catch the revelation that obedience is better than sacrifice (1 Sam. 15:22). In that rebuke—and in Saul's response—we find one way Christians are practicing a sin that is in the realm of witchcraft: via rebellion that arises when the fear of man is greater than the fear of the Lord. Let's look at the exchange:

> "For rebellion is as the sin of witchcraft, and stubbornness is as iniquity and idolatry. Because you have rejected the word of the LORD, He has also rejected you from being king."
>
> Saul said to Samuel, "I have sinned. For I have transgressed the commandment of the LORD, and your words, because I feared the people, and obeyed their voice."
>
> —1 SAMUEL 15:23–24

Unfortunately Saul didn't learn his lesson. He continued disobeying God and eventually lost his kingdom. Fear of man was at the root of his rebellion, but rebellion grows from many roots. If you see rebellion operating in your life, find the root and rip it out!

Then there's Jezebel's witchcraft, which I mentioned briefly. In 2 Kings 9:22, right before the wicked queen's demise, Jehu offered insight into an open door for the Jezebel spirit when he told her son, "What peace, so long as the whoredoms of thy mother Jezebel and her witchcrafts are so many?" (KJV). The spirit of Jezebel is essentially a spirit of seduction that works to escort believers into immorality and idolatry. (See Revelation 2:20.) And this spirit uses witchcraft against its enemies.

Jezebel's witchcraft was rooted in rebellion, but the witchcraft in 2 Kings 9:22 refers to incantations and spells.[6] In the modern church world we call them "word curses." Jezebel released a word curse against Elijah that carried a spirit of fear when she sent him this message after he had killed 450 prophets of Baal in a great display of God's power: "So let the gods do to me and more also, if I do not make your life as the life of one of them by tomorrow about this time" (1 Kings 19:2).

In modern times word curses aren't always so dramatic. When we speak negatively over someone's life—"She will never hold down a job acting like that," "Their marriage is bound to fail the way he treats her," "The doctors said he's going to die in thirty days. Isn't that sad?"—we are agreeing with the enemy's plan and giving power to it with our anointed mouths. The power of death and life are in the tongue. If you are inadvertently—or purposely—releasing witchcraft over people with the words of your mouth, repent and get your mouth back in line with the Spirit of God.

WORKS OF YOUR FLESH

Make no mistake. The Spirit of God is against witchcraft in whatever form it takes, from divination to magic to rebellion to word curses to works of the flesh. Paul explained that the flesh lusts against the Spirit and the Spirit against the flesh (Gal. 5:17). What are the works of the flesh? Galatians 5:19–21 lists them: "adultery, fornication, uncleanness, lasciviousness, idolatry, witchcraft, hatred, variance, emulations, wrath, strife, seditions, heresies, envyings, murders, drunkenness, revellings, and such like" (KJV).

Notice that witchcraft is listed right alongside adultery and fornication. Witchcraft is a serious offense in any manifestation. As a work of the flesh, witchcraft violates the first commandment: "You shall have no other gods before Me" (Exod. 20:3). The flesh opposes the move of the Spirit and resists all things spiritual. This is a serious struggle because Paul assures us that those who practice witchcraft will not inherit the kingdom of God (Gal. 5:21).

If you know you are disobeying God in an area, repent of this sin, which God views in the same way He sees witchcraft, and get back in line with the Spirit. If you are cursing people with your negative words of gossip and death, stop practicing this witchcraft and begin blessing them. If you are flowing in fleshly witchcraft, crucify your flesh with its passions and desires (Gal. 5:24). If you live in the Spirit, walk in the Spirit (v. 25)—and walk free from the practice of witchcraft.

As I mentioned previously, Merriam-Webster's dictionary defines witchcraft as an irresistible influence or fascination—and the Bible warns us not to be bewitched: "O foolish Galatians! Who has bewitched you that you should not obey the truth? Before your eyes Jesus Christ was clearly portrayed among you as crucified" (Gal. 3:1).

Obviously there is a spiritual force the Bible is warning us about. It causes us to take leave of our senses. Witchcraft releases strong confusion against our minds so that Jesus is not the clear focus of our lives. Once that happens, we are more vulnerable to the vain imaginations the enemy whispers to our souls. We have a responsibility to know about this spiritual wickedness and guard ourselves against it.

EIGHT SIGNS WITCHCRAFT IS ATTACKING YOU

With that said, here are eight signs you are under a witchcraft attack right now.

1. Confusion

Witchcraft makes you question yourself, your friends, your leaders—and even God. When witchcraft attacks, it's difficult to make sound decisions. You may forget your keys, important appointments, or even what the Word says.

When strong confusion hits your mind, you can be sure it's not coming from God. God is not the author of confusion but of peace (1 Cor. 14:33).

2. Having trouble paying attention

When witchcraft attacks, it can feel like your mind is scrambled like an egg. You have trouble staying focused on the tasks at hand. Your mind wanders to and fro. You just can't keep a train of thought or pay attention to what you are hearing or reading. It can be difficult to hear from God and discern the devil. We must walk in 1 Peter 5:8: "Be sober and watchful, because your adversary the devil walks around as a roaring lion, seeking whom he may devour."

3. Wanting to hide in your cave

I like my cave. I like being alone with God. But when I feel tempted to hide in my cave rather than face the world—when I feel like David when he said, "Oh, that I had wings like a dove! For then I would fly away and be at rest" (Ps. 55:6)—I know I'm under attack. When Jezebel sent a messenger of fear with a word curse threatening Elijah's life, he ran scared and left his servant behind, sat in a cave, and wished he was dead. That's a witchcraft attack.

4. Forgetting who you really are

You are a child of the King. You are the righteousness of God in Christ Jesus. Greater is He who is in you than he who is in the world (1 John 4:4). You are blessed coming in and blessed going out. Everything you put your hand to prospers. That is your legal position. But when witchcraft attacks, you feel like a worthless worm. You forget who you are in Christ and have little to no interest in the Word, church, praise, worship, or the like. You may feel guilt, condemnation, or self-pity.

5. Feeling discouraged, depressed, and ready to quit

We all get discouraged from time to time, but when witchcraft attacks, you may just want to throw in the towel; send your resignation letter to God; quit, give up, cozy up in bed, and pull the covers over your head. The devil comes to wear you out (Dan. 7:25), yet the Bible commands us not to grow weary in well-doing and promises we will reap a harvest if we don't give up (Gal. 6:9). There's the tension, but let's be clear. The devil is trying to steal your harvest. Don't let him.

6. Feeling angry and frustrated

When witchcraft attacks, you may feel angry and frustrated. You feel like people and things are standing in your way. You may get mad at yourself, the devil, or even God. You're sick and tired of your circumstances, but what you don't realize is that the enemy is magnifying your circumstances with distorted mirrors and smoke that clouds reality. When this happens, just keep acknowledging the Lord. He will make your paths straight (Prov. 3:6, NIV).

7. Experiencing sickness, aches, and pains

I've told you before that when witchcraft attacks me, my eyes burn. Sometimes my chest gets tight and I get dizzy. One of my intercessors gets terrible back pain when witchcraft manifests in her life. Another of my friends sees old stroke symptoms return. Sickness is not from God. We have authority over it, but many times we like to grumble and complain and confess how bad off we are, which only strengthens the enemy's grip on us. The devil brings what Jonah 2:8 calls "lying vanities" (KJV) against you to make you think something is wrong so you'll confess it out of your mouth and open the door for it to settle.

8. Feeling just plain worn out

If you've slept eight hours, had a tall cup of coffee, and you still feel like you've been run over by a truck, witchcraft could be attacking you. This is one of the ways witchcraft comes after me. I've learned not to give in by lying down for a nap that turns into four or five hours of witchcraft-induced sleep. If you are eating well, sleeping well, exercising well, and living well—and if you are generally healthy—you shouldn't feel like you're walking through quicksand. This could be a witchcraft attack.[7]

SEVEN QUESTIONS TO ASK YOURSELF

I am not one to beat the air (1 Cor. 9:26). I don't presume to know what spirit may be attacking me by comparing symptoms to a checklist. Lists like the previous one are meant to prime the pump of information that could spark a revelation. Ultimately we need Holy Spirit discernment to be absolutely sure we're waging warfare against the right demon. The last thing we want to do is provoke another spirit to join forces with the real culprit. We need to put the discernment back into spiritual warfare. In my experience, though, there are some practical questions you can ask yourself to help you discern a witchcraft attack:

1. Are you on an emotional roller coaster, rushing from anger to sadness to confusion? You could be under a witchcraft attack.

2. Are you so overwhelmed with your circumstances that you just want to call in sick, stay in bed, and feel sorry for yourself? You could be under a witchcraft attack.

3. Do you feel like nobody can possibly understand what you are going through and that nobody even cares anyway? You could be under a witchcraft attack.

4. Do you feel like everything you do is wrong, that nobody appreciates you anyway? You could be under a witchcraft attack.

5. Are you getting offended with people? Are you touchy and fretting over what people are doing or saying? You could be under a witchcraft attack.

6. Are people rising up against you with false accusations and angry outbursts without any apparent justification? You could be under a witchcraft attack.

7. Is the way you're thinking about your life making you feel fearful or confused? You could be under a witchcraft attack.

Before I understood the power of witchcraft, I could answer yes to those questions when I was under attack. Witchcraft doesn't hit me that way anymore. In fact, I've learned to take authority over it, cast down imaginations, be slow to speak, and maintain my joy despite the exhaustion, low-grade headaches, and burning eyes.

When that doesn't work, I've learned that when I've done all I can do, to stand. I have learned to open my mouth and ask others to fight with me because one can put a thousand to flight and two can put ten thousand to flight. And I've learned to get into the presence of God and pray in the Spirit. If we submit ourselves to God and resist witchcraft, it will eventually flee. Remember, when you've done all you can do, stand—and just keep standing.

A PRAYER THAT WINS
AGAINST WITCHCRAFT

You can't remain passive when the power of witchcraft is attacking you. Worship will take you a long way in your battles against witchcraft, but depending on how long it has settled upon you, strong prayer is necessary to break totally free. At times you also need to enlist the help of others. Use this prayer starter to get you going:

In the name of Jesus, Father, I come to You and repent of any rebellion or disobedience that opened the door to a witchcraft attack. I submit myself to You fully now. I submit my thoughts to You. I submit my words to You. I submit my heart to You. I submit my physical body to You.

I resist the power of witchcraft that has attacked my body and mind. I resist every symptom of witchcraft, including "mind traffic" and thoughts that exalt themselves against the knowledge of Christ. I resist the fatigue, weariness, and the desire to give up. I resist the strong confusion that has hit my soul. I resist self-pity and feelings of being misunderstood. I resist feeling overwhelmed. I resist the temptation to let my emotions reign. I resist sickness, aches, and pains. I resist discouragement and depression. I resist the attacks against my identity and the enemy's provocation to withdraw. I resist the bait of offense. I stand strong against it in the name of the Lord.

And now, in the name of Jesus, I break every word curse, thought curse, hex, vexation, spell, incantation, potion, and any expression of witchcraft coming against my mind, body, family, finances, and every other area of my life. I break the powers of witchcraft. I take authority over mind-binding and mind-bending spirits and all forms of mind control. I strip witchcraft of its power to harm me. I plead the blood of Jesus over my mind, will, and emotions and ask You to give me greater discernment to resist this power at its onset.

I pray for those who have cursed me and ask You to forgive them whether or not they know what they are doing. Open the eyes of their heart and give them an encounter with Your great love. In Jesus's name, amen.

CHAPTER 7

DEATH'S DANGEROUS STING

PASTOR ROBBY DAWKINS was preaching in a European church when a man suddenly started twitching on the front row. His hand withered up. His mother started screaming for an ambulance. Robby rushed over and started waging war on the spirits attacking the man.

"What I saw was a strong demonic presence over him. His head was contorting and looked to me like it would almost twist, as well as his jaw, face, and hands contorting," Robby told me. "They were drawn up toward his chest and neck. It seemed every muscle was at an extreme strain in his body. He was jerking and twitching severely."

Robby started binding demonic powers and commanding the man's body to be loosed in Jesus's name—but he did not see immediate results. In fact, the man started turning blue as the life-and-death drama escalated rapidly.

"His lips turned from purple to blue-black. It turns out there was a doctor right beside me, and he started praying with me," said Robby, who is pastor of Vineyard Church in Aurora, Illinois. "Several people started gathering around. We laid him on the floor and began to rebuke the spirit of death."

It looked hopeless as the man's pupils became fixed and

dilated. Robby told me he heard the death rattle—the sound a dying person makes when fluids accumulate in the throat and upper chest—and then it stopped. Robby said he had his hand on the man's heart as the doctor checked his pulse. Just by looking at him, the man's mother screamed out, "He's dead. He's dead," and the doctor confirmed there was no pulse.

"As I continued to pray, I began to bind the spirit of death and say, 'You can't have him!' I began to declare the resurrection life of Jesus Christ over him. People were beginning to get a bit restless, but then I could hear his breathing start to recover and his color started to return," Robby said. "His lips that were purplish black started to get less dark. His eyes stopped being fixed and dilated and started to move. We rolled him onto his side at that point to allow his tongue to fall forward, but he was starting to come round."

The man started rolling back and forth, and then did something he couldn't do before the episode—he spoke. See, past strokes had left him unable to speak. This man was not only raised from the dead; his speech was fully restored.

"I turned him toward me and pulled him into my chest—like a hug—and declared a full impartation of life. He let go and then embraced me again," Robby says. "I did this because I had a friend who had raised the dead and said there is something about the chest-to-chest connection—like in the Bible—that seems to impart life. I continued to pray and break off the enemy's assignment against him. Some men helped him to the back of the church to wait for the ambulance."

DISCERNING THE POWER OF DEATH

"O death, where is your sting? O grave, where is your victory?" (1 Cor. 15:55). We know that we will one day trade the corruptible for incorruption, the mortal for immortality (v. 53). God said, "My Spirit will not always strive with man, for he is flesh; yet his days will be a hundred and twenty years" (Gen. 6:3). The psalmist later wrote, "The years of our life are seventy, and if by reason of strength eighty" (Ps. 90:10).

We know that dust returns to the earth and "the spirit returns to God who gave it" (Eccles. 12:7). Although some journeys are much shorter—Jesus died when He was in His thirties, and Stephen was still a young man when he was stoned for preaching the gospel—our times are in God's hands (Ps. 31:15). And Jesus is the resurrection and the life, so natural death is merely a graduation to eternal existence. Our citizenship is in heaven and Jesus has gone to prepare a place for us—but the spirit of death works to take some saints out prematurely so they cannot fulfill their destinies in Christ.

John 10:10 proclaims that Jesus came to give us abundant life but the enemy comes to steal, kill, and destroy. Surely Jesus disarmed principalities and powers, triumphing over them by the Cross (Col. 2:15). But death has not yet been destroyed: "For He will reign until He has put all enemies under His feet. The last enemy that will be destroyed is death" (1 Cor. 15:25–26). Death and Hades will be thrown into the lake of fire, along with those whose names are not written in the Lamb's Book of Life (Rev. 20:14–15).

Meanwhile, the power of death is alive and well in the earth. We see tragic accidents, horrific murders, and otherwise untimely deaths from sickness and disease that I am convinced are not the will of God. If death was always

God's perfect will, we would not see so many people raised from the dead, but the Bible is full of these accounts.

Elijah raised the widow of Zarephath's son from the dead (1 Kings 17:17–22). Elisha raised the Shunammite woman's son from the dead (2 Kings 4:32–35). Elisha's bones raised a man from the dead (2 Kings 13:20–21). Jesus raised the Nain widow's son from the dead (Luke 7:11–15). Jesus raised Jairus's daughter from the dead (Luke 8:41–55). Jesus raised Lazarus from the dead (John 11:1–44). Peter raised Dorcas from the dead (Acts 9:36–41). Paul raised Eutychus from the dead (Acts 20:9–10). If it wasn't God's will to raise them from the dead, He wouldn't have.

Likewise we see modern accounts of the dead being raised—saints who combat the spirit of death and win. Reinhard Bonnke, Heidi Baker, Smith Wigglesworth, William Branham, and others have documented cases of people raised from the dead in their ministry. The power of death is certainly at work to take out saints before their time, and we need to learn to discern its attack and resist it so it cannot prevail.

Hebrews 2:14–15 tells us the devil holds the power of death, but our God is greater: "So then, as the children share in flesh and blood, He likewise took part in these, so that through death He might destroy him who has the power of death, that is, the devil, and deliver those who through fear of death were throughout their lives subject to bondage."

THE WAGES OF SIN IS DEATH

The Bible says the wages of sin is death but the gift of God is eternal life through Christ Jesus (Rom. 6:23). Sin opens the door to death. This death doesn't always manifest as a physical loss of life; it is a power that works to steal, kill, and destroy lives—and dreams. It seeks to steal, kill, and destroy relationships and godly visions you have been given.

Adam and Eve's original sin against God—eating from the tree of the knowledge of good and evil—introduced death into the world. God said, "For in the day that you eat from it you will surely die" (Gen. 2:17). We know they didn't die immediately, and that is part of what makes sin so deceptive. You don't always reap an immediate harvest from the seed of sin you plant. But sin does set in motion a spiritual law. Thank God, we can repent and stop that harvest of death, though there are often still consequences of our sin. Consider Paul the Apostle's teaching in Romans 6:2–14:

> How shall we who died to sin live any longer in it? Do you not know that we who were baptized into Jesus Christ were baptized into His death? Therefore we were buried with Him by baptism into death, that just as Christ was raised up from the dead by the glory of the Father, even so we also should walk in newness of life.
>
> For if we have been united with Him in the likeness of His death, so shall we also be united with Him in the likeness of His resurrection, knowing this, that our old man has been crucified with Him, so that the body of sin might be destroyed, and we should no longer be slaves to sin. For the one who has died is freed from sin.
>
> Now if we died with Christ, we believe that we shall also live with Him, knowing that Christ, being raised from the dead, will never die again; death has no further dominion over Him. For the death He died, He died to sin once for all, but the life He lives, He lives to God.
>
> Likewise, you also consider yourselves to be dead

to sin, but alive to God through Jesus Christ our Lord. Therefore do not let sin reign in your mortal body, that you should obey it in its lusts. Do not yield your members to sin as instruments of unrighteousness, but yield yourselves to God, as those who are alive from the dead, and your bodies to God as instruments of righteousness. For sin shall not have dominion over you, for you are not under the law, but under grace.

Now, just because we are under grace doesn't mean we should sin. God forbid! The point is that as believers we have the opportunity to repent. If we don't repent—if we practice sin despite the Holy Spirit's conviction and choose to continually walk in disobedience to God's revealed will for our lives—the wages of sin will eventually manifest in our lives.

When David sinned with Bathsheba, he did not see the wages of that sin—the death of his firstborn child and the drama in his family line—for some time. Occasionally you don't see the wages of your sin for decades. Other times you see harvest immediately. Be warned: payday will come. Examine your heart for any known sin, especially if you are experiencing chronic illness, suicidal thoughts, hopelessness, a pattern of loss or destruction, dead or dying dreams, or thoughts that say, "I wish I was dead." Those may be signs of a spirit of death attacking your life.

WHAT OPENS THE DOOR TO DEATH'S ATTACK?

Some sins produce death more quickly than others. When Ananias and Sapphira lied to the Holy Spirit in the midst of revival, death immediately overtook them (Acts 5:1–11).

Likewise, when King Herod took glory that belonged to God, death immediately overtook him (Acts 12:23). Usually, though, unrepentant sin is like a cancer that eats away at you slowly.

Unforgiveness, harboring hate in your heart, also can open the door to the spirit of death. Jesus was clear when He said, "Whoever hates his brother is a murderer, and you know that no murderer has eternal life remaining in him" (1 John 3:15).

Another way to open the door to the power of death is to dabble in the occult. Leviticus 20:27 warns that occultism is punishable by death. God is not likely to swiftly strike Christians dead who practice occult behaviors such as seeking mediums or psychics and engaging in other dark practices, but it does set off the law of sin. Curses, cursed objects, and even horror movies and dark music can open the door to the spirit of death.

Note that like any spirit, the power of death may have entered through no fault of your own. It may enter through your bloodline. If there is murder in your bloodline, you need to repent even though you are not the one who committed the murder. Suicide in your family line is another manifestation of death. Generational curses are a common root of the power of death operating in a person's life.

Beyond generational issues, though, you may have unknowingly welcomed the power of death in your life by your thoughts and actions. If you've wished someone was dead, you have committed murder in your heart, as this rises out of hatred. Abortion falls under the category of murder. If you have had an abortion or someone in your family line has had an abortion, it opens the door to death.

Some children are dedicated to evil spirits at birth. This can open the door to all manner of demonic oppression, including and especially the power of death. The spirit of fear can open the door to the spirit of death, especially if it manifests as a fear of dying or a fear of death.

The power of death and life is in the tongue (Prov. 18:21). You can welcome the power of death into your life with the words of your mouth. Indeed, your own words can condemn you. Jesus said, "For by your words you will be justified, and by your words you will be condemned" (Matt. 12:37).

Yes, your words can defile you (Matt. 15:18). The Bible warns us not to let corrupt communication come out of our mouths (Eph. 4:29). Solomon counsels us, "He who guards his mouth preserves his life, but he who opens wide his lips will have destruction" (Prov. 13:3). Colossians 3:8 tells us to put away all obscene talk from our mouths. Our words are so powerful, it would be worth your time to do a good study on the mouth. It will put the fear of the Lord in your heart.

GRIEF'S UNDERHANDED RAID

Most Christians aren't dabbling in the occult or harboring hate in their hearts. Generational curses are easy enough to deal with. And we can learn to guard our mouths with the Holy Spirit's help. But grief is an underhanded strategy the enemy uses to barge in with the power of death and demand our attention.

Merriam-Webster's dictionary first defines grief as a "deep and poignant distress caused by or as if by bereavement."[1] But make no mistake: you don't have to witness a physical death to grieve. Losing a job, home, or a friend can bring grief to your soul. Prolonged suffering can leave you grieving. Hope deferred makes the heart sick (Prov. 13:12). Natural disasters, divorce, poor health, personal injury, imprisonment, a child leaving home, strained relationships, and many other stressful life events can leave you grieving.

I still remember Ralph, who continued grieving his mother's death many years after she passed. Although there are five stages of grief—denial, anger, bargaining, depression, and acceptance—Ralph never accepted his mother's death. He did not receive the comfort Jesus promises those who mourn (Matt. 5:4). After Moses died, the Israelites grieved him for thirty days (Deut. 34:8). I am not suggesting that thirty days is long enough to get through the grieving process, but it shouldn't take years to process either.

Over the years, Ralph grew sicker and sicker. He contracted diabetes. He had heart issues. He was constantly ill. One day the Lord told me that if Ralph did not stop grieving his mother, a spirit of death would overtake him within six months and he would die. It was a shocking word, one that I did not want to hear or share. I finally shared it with his sister, who bore witness to the prophecy and pled with her brother to rise up and stop mourning. He didn't, and he died suddenly of a heart attack in his early fifties.

Again, grief doesn't follow death alone. Grief can come after a major heartbreak, a string of disappointing life experiences, or dying dreams. Grief—deep sadness—can also come in by way of depression. Left unchecked, oppression follows and spirits of infirmity and death begin circling like vultures hovering over a dying animal. We must learn to grieve properly. Acknowledge your loss, cry out to God for His intervention, surround yourself with friends, and if you can't seem to shake the grief, get the help you need before you invite a spirit into your life.

If you discern death attacking you, pray. When the prophet Isaiah told King Hezekiah to get his affairs in order because he would surely die, he cried out to the Lord and was granted another fifteen years (Isa. 38:5; 2 Kings 20:6). David revealed, "When the waves of death encompassed me, the currents of destruction made me afraid. The ropes of Sheol were wrapped around me; the snares of death were opposite me. In my distress I called on the LORD, and cried out to my God; from His temple He heard my voice. My cry reached His ears" (2 Sam. 22:5–7).

A PRAYER TO DRIVE AWAY THE SPIRIT OF DEATH

The spirit of death is sneaky. You need to discern its operations before you can defeat it. Once you are sure you are battling this spirit, you can surely take authority over its operations if you understand the promises of God. Spend some time meditating on God's promises for healing, wholeness, and life before you release this prayer.

Father, I come to You in the name of Jesus and ask You to thwart the plans of the destroyer's death campaign in my life. Forgive me for not discerning death's operations against my life before now. I actively enforce the covenant of life You promised to me. I speak Christ's resurrection life over myself. I proclaim the Holy Spirit's resurrection power in my body. I declare death is under my feet. I thank You, Lord, that You hold the keys of death and hell, and my times are in Your hands. I say I shall not die but live and recount the deeds of the Lord. I say the power of death shall not prosper against my life.

I bind the spirit of death's attacks against my life, my dreams, and my family. I cast the spirit of death far from my dwelling place. I loose Your eternal life in its place. I receive Your breath of life that blows away the residue of death's attacks. I live and move and have my being in Christ, the eternal One. I am alive with Christ. His life is my life. The Spirit that raised Christ from the dead dwells in me and causes me to live abundantly—spirit, soul, and body. The Spirit of life on the inside of me gives me newness of life despite death's agenda. I am free from the bonds of immature death. Whom the Son sets free is free indeed. In Jesus's name, amen.

PART THREE

DEMONS THAT
BRING TORMENT

CHAPTER 8

FEAR'S FALSE FEELINGS

FEAR STARTED RIDDLING my soul when I was a small child. I vividly recall seeing the spirit of fear in my bedroom most nights and screaming for my mother. The spirit I saw in the shadows looked to me like an alligator. My mother came in with a broom and chased it away, thinking it was merely my overactive imagination at work. But it always came back with a vengeance.

As an adult, after I had suffered many traumatic events— some of which I share in chapter 10—fear dominated my life. I was so fearful that if an e-mail came in that I thought might be bad news, I would close my eyes and, with a racing heart, forward it to a friend who could read it for me and filter out the scary parts.

I remember one time I ordered a pizza that seemed to take forever to arrive. So much for the thirty-minute hot and fresh guarantee. I was famished. When the delivery boy finally knocked on the door, it scared me so bad, I locked myself in my bedroom. Then I called to complain that the pizza never showed up.

That's called bondage. Fear's false feelings were no longer just feelings. I had a legion of fear spirits that impacted every area of my life and manifested in diverse ways. I will always remember the day I was set to meet with the deliverance minister who agreed to cast out fear. I had never experienced any deliverance, but I had seen plenty of dramatics at the altar in my short time as a Christian.

I was too scared to go in the church and pondered leaving—the devil will always try to get you to run from freedom—until someone saw me sitting in my car and came out to get me. When I went inside, two ladies took me upstairs to a room with concrete floors and no carpet. I was seriously terrified I'd fall to the ground writhing and crack open my skull. I imagined myself in the hospital. Fear fought for its fortified stronghold in my mind until I repented of agreeing with its voice, renounced it, and commanded it to go—with no wild dramatics. That moment was transformational in my life.

You may not need that level of deliverance, but you certainly wrestle with this powerful force of the wicked one at least from time to time, whether you recognize it or not. Many times fear is so cloaked that you cannot discern it and would deny you're afraid.

Fear comes in times of transition. Fear comes to stop you from advancing in God. Fear comes in the midst of loss. Sometimes fear is so subtle it's hard to trace its root, and this is when it is most difficult to overcome. Make no mistake, fear is your nemesis. It is a master weapon in the enemy's hand that defies God's promises in your life.

DISCERNING THE MANY FACES OF FEAR

Just because I was delivered from the spirit of fear doesn't mean I never have to battle fear. Fear attacks us all at opportune times and will until Jesus comes back. However, understanding how fear is compartmentalized can help you recognize even the subtlest attack.

Remember how I was too afraid to open the door to the pizza man? Seems ridiculous, especially considering I had no fear of traveling to Cuba as an investigative reporter, going glacier flying in Alaska as a travel writer, or launching a freelance writing business in a bad economy. Maybe you're the same way. Maybe you aren't scared to jump out of an airplane but you are petrified of public speaking. Maybe you aren't afraid of public speaking but you are terrified of the dark.

There are literally dozens of diagnosed phobias that demonstrate compartmentalized fear. Some are common and some are so ridiculous you know it has to be the devil, such as fear of flowers, fear of numbers, fear of books, fear of mirrors, fear of clocks, fear of houses, fear of feet, and even fear of fear.

Some people are afraid of spiders; others let tarantulas crawl all over them. Some have a fear of heights; others skydive. Some have a fear of dogs; others are dog lovers. Some have a fear of abandonment; others like to be alone. Many people fear change, tall bridges, sharks, doctors, pain, getting old, the future, or even death.

You may struggle with fear of failure, fear of loss, fear of lack, or even fear of success. If you have a fear failure, you may not even know it because your coping mechanism, your response to it, is subtle and has become part of your personality. So you keep failing because you don't have the faith to succeed. You take action based on your fear instead of based on your faith. It's the same way with any fear. Fear likes to mask itself as anything other than fear so you won't allow God's perfect love to cast it out.

At other times fear reactions are obvious, like me locking

myself in the room when the pizza man came knocking. When Jezebel threatened Elijah, he ran for his life. When Moses killed the Egyptian, he ran to the back side of the desert. They opted for a flight response instead of standing and fighting in faith. Like David with Goliath, we must not run from the battles God has called us to fight—we must run to them knowing we have the victory in Christ. We need a revelation that the good fight of faith Paul told Timothy about is good because we will win it if we run to the battle line. God has not given us a spirit of fear but of power, love, and a sound mind (2 Tim. 1:7).

Know this: Fear has no right to enter our lives. Fear is part of the curse of the law as found in Deuteronomy 28:66, "Your life shall hang in doubt before you. You will be in dread day and night and will have no assurance of your life." The good news is that Jesus redeemed us from the curse of the law by becoming a curse for us (Gal. 3:13).

Faith without action is dead. Fear without action lives. If you don't identify and face your fear, you will not live God's best life for you. By contrast, when you identify your fear you can face it with the sword of the Spirit in your mouth, defeat it, and gain the spoils of war. Victory starts with getting fear out of your mind and out of your mouth. Stop confessing the fearful thoughts the devil whispers to your soul, and you won't fuel the fear.

We have to give fear permission to wreak havoc on our lives. It's time to face your fears. As you read this chapter, I am believing the Holy Spirit will reveal to you any hidden fears plaguing your life so you can confront and conqueror them, and live the abundant life Jesus died to give you. And if you have a fear of confrontation, it's time to overcome that also.

HOW FEAR ENTERS

The Bible tells us over and over to "fear not." In fact, without faith it is impossible to please God (Heb. 11:6). That verse used to leave me feeling condemned, but it's not meant to condemn—it's meant to confront the doubt, unbelief, and fear that wrestles our minds, will, and emotions.

God expects us to take Him at His Word. He tells us He is not a man that He should lie, nor the son of man that He should repent (Num. 23:19). It's insulting to God when we believe what the devil says over what He says. That's why He is not pleased with unbelief—but even in that He remains committed to you.

If you look in the Old Testament, God didn't even want fearful people in His army. Remember Gideon? After the Lord worked the unbelief out of him, He had to separate the fearful soldiers from Gideon's army before the battle against the Midianites because He didn't want them to make bad decisions when the pressure was on. The army shrunk from 32,000 to a meager 300, and God got the glory for the victory (Judg. 7). Now we're all soldiers in the army of God, and He is not about to kick us out, but He does want to kick out the spirit of fear.

So how does fear come? The same way faith comes, essentially. Romans 10:17 tells us, "Faith comes by hearing, and hearing by the word of God." Fear comes by hearing the voice of the enemy, by meditating on and talking about the devil's words. Faith and fear are both spiritual powers. They operate according to the same spiritual law.

Mark 11:23 says, "For truly I say to you, whoever says to this mountain, 'Be removed and be thrown into the sea,' and does not doubt in his heart, but believes that what he says will come to pass, he will have whatever he says." If you have fear in your heart and believe what you say will come to pass, you will have whatever you say. Our words are containers of power. We can release the power of death or life over ourselves (Prov. 18:21). It's our choice.

Fear contaminates our faith and delivers a rotten harvest in our lives. Remember Job's "just in case" offerings for the sin of his children? Job admitted, "For the thing which I greatly feared has happened to me, and that which I dreaded has come to me" (Job 3:25). It went downhill for Job as his fear opened a door to the enemy's destruction. Fear works the same way in our lives. Fear and faith run along parallel lines, but one is faith in God and the other is faith in the devil. We have to make a choice about what we think. Jesus taught:

> No one can serve two masters. For either he will hate the one and love the other, or else he will hold to the one and despise the other. You cannot serve God and money.
>
> Therefore, I say to you, take no thought about your life, what you will eat, or what you will drink, nor about your body, what you will put on. Is not life more than food and the body than clothing? Look at the birds of the air, for they do not sow, nor do they reap, nor gather into barns. Yet your heavenly Father feeds them. Are you not much better than they? Who among you by taking thought can add a cubit to his stature?
>
> Why take thought about clothing? Consider the lilies of the field, how they grow: They neither work, nor do they spin. Yet I say to you that even Solomon in all his glory was not dressed like one of these. Therefore, if God so clothes the grass of the field, which today is here and tomorrow is thrown

into the oven, will He not much more clothe you, O you of little faith? Therefore, take no thought, saying, "What shall we eat?" or "What shall we drink?" or "What shall we wear?" (For the Gentiles seek after all these things.) For your heavenly Father knows that you have need of all these things. But seek first the kingdom of God and His righteousness, and all these things shall be given to you. Therefore, take no thought about tomorrow, for tomorrow will take thought about the things of itself. Sufficient to the day is the trouble thereof.

—MATTHEW 6:24–34

See, Jesus was warning them not to accept fearful thoughts because the enemy ultimately works in our thought life. Devastating circumstances or just bad days may happen, but how we process those devastations and bad days matters. We can frame our lives with faith or fear. The enemy always comes with fearful questions: "How are you going to handle this one? What are you going to do now? Why did God let this happen? Are you sure God told you to step out and do this?" As it was in the Garden of Eden, the devil's questions aim to deceive us into doubt, unbelief, and ultimately fear. Acting on fear unleashes its ultimate power in your life.

What are you worrying about? Listen to the thoughts; think about what you're thinking about. Listen to the words that are coming out of your mouth. Ask your friends to help you catch your fearful statements. Pay attention to the types of situations and people you tend to avoid. Discern behaviors that faith doesn't inspire. Catch yourself comparing yourself with others. Look out for perfectionism. Notice when you settle for less or say no when you want to say yes, or say yes when you want to say no. Beware of procrastination and tendencies to withdraw, run, or try to control situations.

DETERMINE TO FEAR THE LORD

Fear could be blocking the answers to your prayers. Fear could be keeping your healing from manifesting. Fear could be blocking that new job opportunity God wants to give you. Fear could be delaying prophetic words from coming to pass. The devil wants us to fear him more than we fear God, which is why we must cultivate the fear of the Lord in our hearts. When we fear the Lord, we will choose to believe Him and reject fear's voice. Consider a few of the promises associated with the fear of the Lord:

- "The fear of the LORD prolongs days" (Prov. 10:27).

- "The fear of the LORD [leads] to life, and he who has it will abide satisfied; he will not be visited with evil" (Prov. 19:23).

- "By humility and the fear of the LORD are riches, and honor, and life" (Prov. 22:4).

- "Happy is the man who always fears, but he who hardens his heart will fall into mischief" (Prov. 28:14).

- "He will bless those who fear the LORD, both the small and great ones" (Ps. 115:13).

- "The angel of the LORD camps around those who fear Him, and delivers them" (Ps. 34:7).

- "Surely His salvation is near to them who fear Him" (Ps. 85:9).

- "The LORD takes pleasure in those who fear Him, in those who hope in His mercy" (Ps. 147:11).

There are many great and mighty promises for provision, protection, and deliverance for those who choose to fear the Lord—who choose to have a reverential respect for Him— and reject the enemy's fear-mongering lies. In His mercy God has even made a way of escape from the clutches of fear. We can repent and choose to believe, and He will rescue us. It's the truth that sets you free and guards you from deception in the first place.

If you are struggling with fear, meditate on these scriptures:

> Even though I walk through the valley of the shadow of death, I will fear no evil; for You are with me; Your rod and Your staff, they comfort me.
> —PSALM 23:4

> The LORD is my light and my salvation; whom will I fear? The LORD is the strength of my life; of whom will I be afraid?
> —PSALM 27:1

> I sought the LORD, and He answered me, and delivered me from all my fears.
> —PSALM 34:4

> Surely His salvation is near to them who fear Him, that glory may dwell in our land.
> —PSALM 85:9

Teach me Your way, O LORD, that I will walk in Your truth; bind my heart to fear Your name.

—PSALM 86:11

For as the heavens are high above the earth, so great is His mercy toward those who fear Him.

—PSALM 103:11

Like a father shows compassion to his children, so the LORD gives compassion to those who fear Him.

—PSALM 103:13

He will fulfill the desire of those who fear Him; He also will hear their cry and will save them.

—PSALM 145:19

Do not fear, for I am with you; do not be dismayed, for I am your God. I will strengthen you, I will help you, yes, I will uphold you with My righteous right hand.

—ISAIAH 41:10

There is no fear in love, but perfect love casts out fear, because fear has to do with punishment.

—1 JOHN 4:18

FACING FEAR'S FEROCIOUS ATTACKS—AND WINNING

Fear is not a once-and-for-all battle, but you can be free from the spirit of fear's stronghold in your mind. You can take authority over fear when it tries to rise up against your soul. You can resist fear and it will indeed flee. Use this prayer starter to help you combat fear's ferocious attack:

Father, in the name of Jesus I come to You repenting of giving in to feelings of fear, heeding the voice of fear, or otherwise cooperating with fear's assignment against my destiny. Thank You for forgiving me and strengthening me to stand against this spirit in all truth and resisting fear's lies. I command fear to loose my thoughts. I rebuke the spirit of fear that is working to entrap me, steal my faith, rob my peace, and otherwise riddle me with anxiety, in Christ's name.

I thank You that I have been redeemed from the curse of the law—and the curse of fear. Give me a greater revelation of Your perfect love that casts out all fear so I can withstand fear's attacks in the evil day. Thank You that You translated me out of fear's dark grip and into the marvelous light of Your liberty. I stake a claim on what belongs to me in the Spirit even now. I declare that You have not given me a spirit of fear but of power, love, and a sound mind.

I command fear to leave my family, my home, and my workplace. I proclaim that fear runs from me. I choose faith, trust, and love. I fear and trust the Lord only, in the name of the Christ. Amen.

CHAPTER 9

JUDAS'S BETRAYING BLUEPRINTS

I'M A TRUSTING person. I don't throw discernment out the window when I encounter new people, but neither do I enter into new relationships with suspicion. Essentially I choose to believe the best, to take people at their word, and to give people the benefit of the doubt. To put it another way, I trust people until they betray my trust.

Most of the time this mind-set lays a foundation for strong relationships. Sometimes, though, you get blindsided by someone you thought you could trust. If you've heard my testimony, you know my husband abandoned me and my two-year-old daughter to marry a woman about half his age in another nation. But that's just a taste of the betrayal I've faced. Indeed, the Judas spirit has risen up against me time and time again.

Once a Christian contractor—a very close friend—left me without a kitchen or any bathrooms on Christmas. He ran off with $10,000 of my cash for a celebration with his family, never to return. Another time, one of my very dearest friends convinced me to pay for a good chunk of her wedding and plan her showers and receptions under the guise that I was the maid of honor, only to find out a week before the wedding that I was not the maid of honor. Yes, I am very familiar with the Judas spirit.

Still, I would rather operate with an open, discerning heart than a closed, suspicious soul. I've learned to discern the treacherous Judas spirit through painful experiences. We have to remember what Paul teaches in Ephesians 6— we're not wrestling against flesh and blood. We are wrestling against spirits that work through people. In the case of the Judas spirit, it works through people who don't trust God to provide what they need—and it almost always blindsides you.

Betrayal can take many forms. Merriam-Webster's dictionary defines it as "to give information about (a person, group, country, etc.) to an enemy; to hurt (someone who trusts you, such as a friend or relative) by not giving help or by doing something morally wrong; to show (something, such as a feeling or desire) without wanting or trying to."[1]

It's no accident that this same dictionary defines "Judas" as "one who betrays under the guise of friendship."[2]

It's interesting that another word for peephole is "judas hole" because it lets you see someone without them seeing you.[3] Someone operating in a Judas spirit usually has keen insight into your life. They know things about you that others don't know. They are close to you—but unless you discern that this spirit is operating, you won't anticipate the wicked plot being forged against you.

HOW THE JUDAS SPIRIT ENTERS YOUR BETRAYER

I could go on and on about the betrayals I have endured and forgiven. A spiritual mother whom I loved dearly betrayed me because she was walking in step with abusive church politics. A spiritual father betrayed me because I refused to bow to his control any longer. I believe the Judas spirit is rising in the end times. Jesus Himself warned, "The brother will deliver up the brother to death, and the father the child. And the children will rise up against their parents and cause them to be put to death" (Matt. 10:21).

Whether a cheating spouse, a broken vow, or an abandoned friendship, betrayals are usually devastating to one degree or another because you would not put your trust in someone you thought would ever dare to hurt you on purpose. Sometimes understanding why a Judas spirit has risen up against you helps you overcome the attack—or at least lessens the sting if you've been blindsided.

Many times offense is involved in betrayal. Indeed, it often activates a Judas spirit's attack. Jesus said that in the end times many "will be offended, will betray one another, and will hate one another" (Matt. 24:10, NKJV). I believe it often happens in that order. People will not betray you unless they first take Satan's bait of offense. And no betrayal stings worse than a knife in your back wielded by someone who was supposed to have your back.

Shakespeare's tragic play *Julius Caesar* makes it clear how the bitter act of betrayal seeks to harm its victim. We remember Caesar's words: "Et tu, Brute?" Jesus put it another way: "Judas, do you betray the Son of Man with a kiss?" (Luke 22:48). And David explained, "Yes, my own close friend, in whom I trusted, who ate of my bread, has lifted up the heel against me" (Ps. 41:9).

Yes, offense opens the door to betrayal, but that's not the only root. Sometimes a person's motives are not right to begin with. They may be greedy for gain. Think of the drug addict who is compelled to steal from his mom to pay for his habit. Think of the businessman who embezzles money from the company who gave him his big break. Similarly, lust can cause someone to betray a significant other. Some people are manipulators who get close to you because they want something, even if it's just the sick and twisted pleasure of playing with your mind and emotions. Other times people change. People may start off with the best intentions toward you until the enemy finds something in them—whether it's personal ambition, fear of loss, or a demonic accusation against your character—and pulls their strings like a puppet master. Still other times they think they can't trust you and decide to get you before you can get them.

CHARACTERISTICS OF THE JUDAS SPIRIT

Although I don't pretend to know everything about the Judas spirit—or any other spirit—I have learned it carries some clearly identifiable characteristics. Those operating in a Judas spirit:

Lack the fruit of the Spirit

Galatians 5:22–23 tells us, "But the fruit of the Spirit is love, joy, peace, patience, gentleness, goodness, faith, meekness, and self-control; against such there is no law." The biblical Judas did not walk in love. He did not care for the needs of the poor. He was selfish and self-centered. Remember, it was Judas who objected when Mary poured perfume on Jesus that could have been sold for money (John 12:5).

Hide their true motives

In the John 12 incident, when Mary anointed Jesus with expensive perfume, Judas wasn't concerned with the poor as he feigned. He was concerned with his own security. The Bible says, "He said this, not because he cared for the poor, but because he was a thief. And having the money box, he used to steal what was put in it" (John 12:6).

Love money

From this incident in John 12 we also learn that greed can open the door to a Judas spirit. The love of money is the root of all evil (1 Tim. 6:10).

Operate in a critical spirit

The fruit of the Spirit is joy, but the biblical Judas never once demonstrated joy. Rather, we see again in the John 12 event how Judas is critical of how Jesus operates His ministry.

Demonstrate a superior, haughty attitude

As treasurer, Judas had an important position in Jesus's earthly ministry. Judas had a haughty spirit. He complained about gifts being given to Jesus because he wanted to take everything of value for himself (John 12:1–7).

Align with your accusers

The Pharisees wanted to kill Jesus, and Judas ultimately helped them. A Judas will eventually align with your accusers and persecutors and help them accomplish their murderous agenda against your reputation by offering them private, often exaggerated information.

Are quick to sell you out

Judas sold Jesus to the Pharisees for thirty pieces of silver. He led Jesus's opponents right to where He was praying in the Garden of Gethsemane (Matt. 26:36–46). This also demonstrates Judas's love of money.

Are hypocritical pretenders

Judas pledged allegiance to Jesus yet betrayed Him. Judas pretended to be something he wasn't—loyal.

From all this you see that a person operating in a Judas spirit can talk the talk and walk the walk. They may labor right alongside you, as Judas did. They may cast out devils and heal the sick, as Judas did. They may break bread with you, as Judas did. They may have an intimate relationship with you, as Judas did. But their hearts are not with you, at least not anymore. They may honor you publicly—Judas kissed Jesus on the cheek in the very moment of the betrayal—but they hold disdain in their hearts.

Scripture describes Judas as a traitor (Luke 6:16). He's called the son of perdition (John 17:12), predicting his sentence to hell after death. He walked with Jesus for three years. He saw miracles, signs, and wonders—but that did not change his heart. He was part of a chosen tribe to run with Jesus on the earth, but that wasn't enough. He rejected the truths Jesus taught repeatedly instead of allowing the Holy Spirit to work in his heart. If people won't repent and are bent on bringing destruction in our lives, we must cut ties and pray for them as the Holy Spirit leads.

WHEN TRUST IS BETRAYED

Jesus knew who would betray Him, but we don't usually see a betrayal coming. Sometimes betrayal blindsides us—but then again, shouldn't we expect it?

People outside your inner circle persecute and malign you, but they can't really betray you because betrayal implies trust. People inside your inner circle—those you've trusted and invested yourself in—can and sometimes do betray you, then they persecute and malign you to disguise their dirty deeds. Sometimes they repent but usually not until later—much later. Of course, we have to forgive them whether they repent or not.

The Holy Spirit once reminded me of this truth after I was blindsided by a betrayal. I started getting calls from people telling me someone who had walked out on the ministry was now making "offhand" comments about me. The Judas was savvy enough not to come right out and speak condemning words, but anyone who could read between the lines could smell the stench of gossip. Because I've been betrayed a number of times, it caused me to go into prayer for my persecutor. That's when I heard the Holy Spirit remind me of His Word with a rhythmic phrase that is so easy to remember: "If you want God to vindicate, don't retaliate!"

That made me smile. In an instant the Holy Spirit began to bring to my remembrance the times I've handled betrayal His way and then saw the fruit of walking in His Word in this area of my life. The Word of God says, "Beloved, do not avenge yourselves, but rather give place to wrath; for it is written, 'Vengeance is Mine, I will repay,' says the Lord. Therefore 'If your enemy is hungry, feed him; if he is thirsty, give him a drink; for in so doing you will heap coals of fire on his head.' Do not be overcome by evil, but overcome evil with good" (Rom. 12:19–21, NKJV).

LIBERTY THROUGH THE SERMON ON THE MOUNT

That passage from Romans 12 will liberate you if you will heed it. But do you need more? Consider the liberty found in these words from the Sermon on the Mount:

> You have heard that it was said, "You shall love your neighbor and hate your enemy." But I say to you, love your enemies, bless those who curse you, do good to those who hate you, and pray for those who spitefully use you and persecute you, that you may be sons of

your Father who is in heaven. For He makes His sun rise on the evil and on the good and sends rain on the just and on the unjust. For if you love those who love you, what reward do you have? Do not even the tax collectors do the same?

—MATTHEW 5:43–46

I learned all of this early in my Christian walk because I came into the faith after two major, life-changing betrayals. Hear me on this. When you are betrayed, you have two choices: you can sink to your hater's level and enjoy the temporary satisfaction of attacking them in the same spirit that attacked you (you can open yourself up to a bitter spirit), or you can decide to move in the opposite spirit—the Spirit of Christ—and allow Him to prepare a table before you in the presence of your enemies (Ps. 23:5).

I've discovered that when I do things God's way, He restores what the enemy stole and promotes me to another level of influence. It happens every time. You just have to hang on to the Word and move on with your life—forgiving your betrayer, opening your heart to receiving God's healing, and then forgetting what lies behind and expecting God to move on your behalf.

HOLD OUT FOR GOD'S VINDICATION

I appeared on Sid Roth's *It's Supernatural!* television show talking about some of my betrayals and how God restored my life, but the radio broadcast offers even more details. On the radio I told the story of leaving a publishing company and how I was sorely betrayed and persecuted on my way out the door—and even years later.

Many people there thought I was in rebellion and deceived. I chose not to retaliate and waited for God to vindicate. I forgave them. He healed me. He promoted me—and then one of the sweetest vindications came nearly four years later through a phone call from an elderly woman still inside the organization. She told me, "I am so proud of you. Everyone thought you were deceived, but God has confirmed you. You followed God out of this place, and look where He has taken you!"

Beloved, don't try to defend yourself. Don't try to make people understand your side of the story. Don't engage in conversation with other people about the betrayal. It doesn't matter what people think. It matters what God thinks. And if God wants to show them the truth, He will do it. Trust God. Let Him pull the knife out of your back. When you refuse to retaliate, God will vindicate! Whether you see that vindication immediately or it takes years, hold on to these words from Romans 8:33–37:

> Who shall bring a charge against God's elect? It is God who justifies. Who is he who condemns? It is Christ who died, and furthermore is also risen, who is even at the right hand of God, who also makes inter-cession for us. Who shall separate us from the love of Christ? Shall tribulation, or distress, or persecution, or famine, or nakedness, or peril, or sword? As it is written: "For Your sake we are killed all day long; we are accounted as sheep for the slaughter." Yet in all these things we are more than conquerors through Him who loved us.
>
> —NKJV

WALKING OUT PSALM 37

Finally, if you've been betrayed, you have to forgive. If you are discerning that you can't trust the people around you,

you have to lean in to Psalm 37. Sometimes you need to emotionally detach, walk in love, and embrace Psalm 37 at a new level. The Holy Spirit told me once, "Trust in the Lord and do good." Consider some of the rest of this psalm and let it encourage your heart:

> Do not fret because of evildoers, nor be jealous of those who do injustice. For they will quickly wither like the grass, and fade like the green herbs. Trust in the LORD, and do good; dwell in the land, and practice faithfulness. Delight yourself in the LORD, and He will give you the desires of your heart.
>
> Commit your way to the LORD; trust also in Him, and He will bring it to pass. He will bring forth your righteousness as the light, and your judgment as the noonday. Rest in the LORD, and wait patiently for Him; do not fret because of those who prosper in their way, because of those who make wicked schemes.
>
> Let go of anger, and forsake wrath; do not fret—it surely leads to evil deeds. For evildoers will be cut off, but those who hope in the LORD will inherit the earth.
>
> —PSALM 37:1–9

I don't know about you, but that changes everything for me. God is our vindicator. We can't always trust people, but we can certainly always trust Him.

A PRAYER TO SEND JUDAS PACKING

The best-case scenario is to betray the Judas spirit's assignment before it has the opportunity to betray you. That doesn't always happen, but we can learn from our mistakes and thwart its next assignment. Pray this prayer to help guard you against the Judas spirit's attack:

Father, I come to You boldly in Jesus's name, asking for forgiveness of my sins and cleansing from all unrighteousness. If I have opened the door for a Judas spirit to work through me, I renounce it in the name of Jesus.

Jesus knew from the beginning who would betray Him. You did not hide it from Him. Father, give me greater discernment about this spirit's operation. Help me see its maneuvers so I can respond appropriately and try to help the betrayer find healing and peace before he takes actions that grieve Your heart. Father, surround me with people who are loyal and true with watchful hearts who can help me see what I can't see.

Father, teach me how to recognize these traits emerging in myself or others in seed form so they don't take root in the hearts of good people who love You. I forgive the Judases who have risen up against me in the past, and I ask You to forgive them, show mercy on them, and bless them. Heal me from any wounds known or unknown from this wicked spirit of betrayal.

Now I break and bind the operation of every Judas spirit coming against my life, my family, my friends, my finances, my ministry, and anything else You've given me to steward. I push back this dark spirit and command it to bow to the name of Jesus. Lord, expose the Judas spirits operating in my midst before they can do more damage to Your kingdom purposes or to my heart. In Jesus's name, amen.

CHAPTER 10

THE BAIT OF BITTERNESS

I WAS STEWING IN my own juices. My husband had abandoned me with a two-year-old and tons of debt so he could suddenly start a new life with a woman about half his age in a foreign nation. I was shocked and dismayed. I was enraged and vengeful. I was bitter—beyond bitter—and it didn't take the gift of discerning of spirits to see it.

I would tell anyone who would listen what a low-down, dirty, good-for-nothing, cheating infidel my husband was. When the grocer at the checkout line asked me how I was, I would share my sad story. When my hairdresser asked me how things were going, I would tell my depressing tale. I was always ready to rehearse and rehash the devastating wrong. I hated him, and I was mad at God.

I felt justified in my stance. After all, there was no excusing what he did, though one of his friends actually tried. I felt righteous in my indignation. I felt morally justified in my rage. And it was eating away at my soul. It was poisoning my life. Worse than pouring salt on a wound, stewing in bitterness, resentment, and unforgiveness was like throwing acid on my already raw emotions.

Within a year I faced another betrayal that landed me in jail for a crime I did not commit. I was beaten and bruised by a bad cop along the way. A close friend took a financial reward for the betrayal, kind of like Judas did. That left me more vengeful than ever as I plotted and planned on that jail bunk how I would repay every enemy who was working to destroy my life. Of course, I had no idea this was all Satan's plot at work.

I didn't know it at the time, but my jail time was prophetic. My natural imprisonment was merely a manifestation of my spiritual imprisonment. When the jailers shackled my hands and feet to transport me, it was a mirror of the spiritual shackles that were binding me. In that jail I got saved—truly saved. Immediately and supernaturally I forgave. I began to take pity on those who had persecuted me, falsely accused me, and abused me. I began praying for those who despitefully used me—without ever having heard the Sermon on the Mount.

When I surrendered to the Lord and released those whom the devil used to try to kill, steal, and destroy my life, the Lord took pity on me. My heavenly Father started fulfilling the Romans 8:28 promise to work all things together for my good. He vindicated me of the false charges, and I was set free on day forty, the number associated with trials in the Bible. I was a new creation in Christ. Old things really did pass away; all things really were new (2 Cor. 5:17).

You may not ever be abandoned and jailed, but you will have opportunities to get offended, resentful, and bitter in your life—many times. How you respond to mistreatment is one of the most important aspects of your spiritual life. When we respond the right way, we climb higher—or go deeper—in the Spirit. When we respond the wrong way, we get bitter. Over time, that bitterness will defile our spirits and dull our ability to sense the presence of God or hear His voice. Bitterness is deadly, and it's easy for the people around you to discern. Where true humility lives, though, bitterness can't take up residence.

BIBLICAL WARNINGS ABOUT BITTERNESS

Resentment, bitterness, and unforgiveness are related—and the Bible has plenty to say about this trio of tormenters. First, let's distinguish between these three emotions that open the door to slaughtering spirits that will wreck your walk with God. The following definitions come from Merriam-Webster's dictionary.

Resentment is "a feeling of indignant displeasure or persistent ill will at something regarded as a wrong, insult, or injury."[1] The residue of resentment builds up over time if we are not quick to forgive. Once when I was in prayer the Lord showed me three people I had resentment against and I didn't even consciously know it. You can also be resentful toward places and things.

Bitterness is associated with being angry or unhappy because of unfair treatment that causes painful emotions felt or experienced in a strong and unpleasant way.[2]

To forgive is "to stop feeling anger toward (someone who has done something wrong); to stop blaming (someone); to stop requiring payment."[3] It is, in essence, to give up resentment. You might say resentment opens the door to bitterness and only forgiveness can slam it shut. The Bible commands us to forgive and warns us what will happen if we don't: we will be delivered to the torturers (Matt. 18:21–35). Unforgiveness gives the enemy a right to torture, torment, and trouble your soul—and believe me, the devil will take advantage.

The writer of Hebrews warned, "Pursue peace with all people, and holiness, without which no one will see the

Lord: looking carefully lest anyone fall short of the grace of God; lest any root of bitterness springing up cause trouble, and by this many become defiled" (Heb. 12:14–15, NKJV).

The Greek word translated "bitterness" in Hebrews 12:15 means "extreme wickedness; a bitter root, and so producing a bitter fruit; bitter hatred." [4] Bitterness is extremely wicked in the eyes of the Lord and correlates to hatred. It's no wonder that bitterness opens the door to demonic oppression. The bitter heart is a darkened heart. First John 2:11 says, "But whoever hates his brother is in darkness, and walks in darkness, and does not know where he is going, because the darkness has blinded his eyes."

Bitterness, then, is connected to spiritual blindness and deception. That's why Paul warns the church at Ephesus to "let all bitterness, wrath, anger, outbursts, and blasphemies, with all malice, be taken away from you. And be kind one to another, tenderhearted, forgiving one another, just as God in Christ also forgave you" (Eph. 4:31–32).

The enemy will set you up to get bitter, feeding your mind with the offense over and over again until you take the bait. Once you bite down on the bribe, the devil has a hook in you and will pull on your mind, will, and emotions. Bitterness will break your heart, bully your soul, and beat its hateful drum in your spiritual ears until it defiles you.

BEWARE THE SPIRIT OF OFFENSE

Bitterness isn't always tied to major offenses. I have witnessed believers getting offended over slight corrections, unreturned phone calls, and even the way certain people say "Holy Spirit." I've heard about believers getting offended over new relationships forming, being asked to sit out travel trips, or not being invited into a back-room meeting.

The Spirit of God showed me clearly that these aren't isolated incidents. There is an actual spirit rising that is causing these unreasonable offenses that open the door to bitterness. It is Satan's plot to divide believers in an hour of church history when it may be more vital than ever for the body of Christ to unite on our common beliefs. When I asked the Lord about this, He explained what is going on:

A spirit of offense is rising and running rampant through the church. Those who are easily offended are candidates for the great falling away. Those who cultivate and maintain an unoffendable heart will escape many of the assignments the enemy will launch in the days to come.

For My people must band together in this hour and refuse to allow petty arguments and soulish imaginations to separate them. This is the time to press into community and relationship and reject the demonic notions and wisdom the enemy is pouring out.

The love of many is waxing cold. Brother is turning against brother and sister against sister in My body. You must come to the unity of the faith in order to accomplish what I've called you to do in this hour. The time is upon you. The opportunity is before you. Lay aside the resentment, bitterness, and unforgiveness and, as far as it depends upon you, seek peace with all men.

Humble yourselves even among those whom you feel are your enemies, and I will work to bring reconciliation that sets the scene for unity from which the anointing flows. You need My anointing to combat the antichrist spirits rising in this hour.

Many of My people are wrestling in their flesh, engaging in works of the flesh, and otherwise letting the flesh lead in battle—and they are battling flesh instead of the spirits influencing the flesh. This is the result of offense. Forgive, let go, embrace your brothers and sisters despite their flaws and sins. I have.

How can you tell if you are easily offended? Here are some markers: you are quick to argue and defend yourself, you are quick to anger, you get your feelings hurt easily, you keep playing comments or actions over and over in your mind and growing resentful, or you don't want to talk to a certain person anymore.

Remember, love is not touchy or easily provoked (1 Cor. 13:5–6). We know that "good sense makes one slow to anger, and it is his glory to overlook an offense" (Prov. 19:11, ESV). And Ecclesiastes offers some really good advice: "Do not give heed to everything people say, lest you hear your servant cursing you. Your heart knows that many times you have spoken a curse against others" (Eccles. 7:21–22). Ultimately, if you are offended, the only way to escape that trap is to spit out the bait. Forgive.

WHEN CHRISTIANS HURT YOU

We expect to be mistreated in the world, but we're often blindsided—and get our feelings hurt—when brothers and sisters in Christ don't invite us to the party, talk behind our backs, or aren't there for us in a time of need. If we're not careful, that can lead us into bitterness.

When a pastor or a parishioner hurts you, the very first action to take is prayer. The hurt you feel is real, and pretending like you aren't hurt isn't going to bring healing. Sometimes when we get hurt in church, folks like to tell us we have no reason to feel bad and we just need to get over it. Half of that statement is true. We do need to get over it, but it's not always true that we have no reason to feel bad. If someone is spewing malicious gossip behind your back and you find out about it, it stings.

No matter what kind of hurt you're dealing with, don't rush into a confrontation with the offender. Take it to God in prayer. Psalm 50:15 says, "Call on Me in the day of trouble." That works for a troubled soul just as well as it does any other trouble. Tell Him how you feel and ask Him to heal your wounds. It may be that the Lord is going to deal with the offender directly and anything you say would just make matters worse. Or, it could be that the Lord will give you a graceful way to explain why you feel hurt. If you take it to God, He can give you the very words to say to your offender (Luke 12:12). And He can bring conviction to that person's heart when you approach him or her in a spirit of humility (John 16:8).

Whatever you do, don't retaliate. In His Sermon on the Mount, Jesus teaches us to turn the other cheek (Matt. 5:39) and to love our enemies, bless those who curse us, do good to those who hate us, and pray for those who spitefully use and persecute us (v. 44).

With that in mind, don't go around telling everybody what someone did to hurt you. And don't make accusations against those who hurt you if you decide to confront the matter. Instead of saying "You hurt my feelings!," say, "When you did that I felt hurt" or "When you talk to me like that I feel upset." Own your feelings because they are your feelings. It's very possible that your offender has no idea that what he said or did hurt you, and never meant to hurt you. If you approach the person in humility seeking reconciliation, your offender may be quick to apologize.

Peter exhorts us to "above all things, have unfailing love for one another, because love covers a multitude of sins"

(1 Pet. 4:8). It could be that the Lord is working something out in you. Maybe you're too sensitive. We always need to check our hearts. Is the person really being hurtful, or are we looking at it through filters of past hurts, rejection, or anger that cloud the truth? Ask the Lord. Or it could be that the Holy Spirit will bring conviction—maybe even heap coals of fire on the offender's head—as you bless him outwardly with a heart of love.

YOU CAN'T HEAL UNTIL YOU FORGIVE

The bottom line is this: it doesn't matter how wrong your offender is; you have to forgive. Forgiveness is not for the other person—it's for you. Forgiveness doesn't justify what someone did that was wrong, nor does it necessarily mean the relationship goes right back to where it was.

If you don't forgive, you end up bitter and resentful, and before too long you'll end up hurting other people. The healing process can't really begin until you spit out the bait of offense. I'll leave you with this prophetic insight the Holy Spirit gave me once when I was extremely hurt in church:

> When the feeling of hurt arises, the spirit of offense comes on the scene to fortify the pain, tempting you to hold on to the grudge in your heart. Therefore, the proper response to emotional pain of the soul is always an immediate confession of forgiveness from the heart. The alternative to forgiveness from the heart is the ongoing torment of the soul. So if you want to be free from your hurts and wounds, take thoughts of forgiveness, meditate on them, and confess them rather than taking thoughts of the hurt, meditating on them, and confessing them. This is God's way—and it's the only way that brings true healing. And while you are

at it, pray for those who have hurt you. This process will cleanse your heart and renew your mind. And you will walk free from the pain of your past.

WHEN YOU'RE BITTER TOWARD GOD

Satan is sometimes called the accuser of the brethren (Rev. 12:10), but I've discovered he is also an accuser of almighty God. Satan will do anything he can to drive a wedge between you and your loving Creator. He points a finger at God when tragedy—or even just a circumstance you don't like—strikes. He suggests God doesn't care about your problems. He blames God for not healing your sick loved one.

All of these accusations come as subtle suggestions—whispers to your soul that intend to make you bitter toward God because you feel disappointed, disillusioned, or deceived. Nothing is ever God's fault, but the devil can surely introduce doubt, ask a well-timed question, or arrange circumstantial evidence to set God up. Don't fall for it. Satan is trying to get you to turn your back on the One who can help you through the disappointment, disillusionment, and deception.

If you are holding a grudge against God, He is ready to deliver you from the gall of bitterness. He's not mad at you, even though you've been mad at Him.

If you find yourself mad at God, do what you would do if you found yourself angry with your spouse or a family member. Get it out in the open. I've shaken my fist at God once and been furiously angry with Him at least one other time. I can tell you this: He would much prefer that you talk to Him about it than shut Him out. If you communicate with God, even if you are angry, He can reach you, help you, and heal you.

Ultimately we need to repent for buying into the devil's lies and accusations against God. But often that repentance won't come at a heart level until we've wrestled with God through the feelings of disappointment, disillusionment, and deception. So if you are mad at God, be honest with Him. It's not like He doesn't already know it. Give Him your anger, and He will turn that anger into peace and a greater revelation of His sovereignty if you will let Him.

A PRAYER TO BREAK THE BACK OF BITTERNESS

Are you ready to let go? Really let go? Lift up this petition to heaven and walk free:

> *Lord, I choose to forgive those who hurt me, offended me, abused me, despitefully used me, or wronged me, my family, and my friends in any way, shape, or form. I ask You also to forgive them and release them from the affront against my soul. Father, forgive them for they know not what they do. Bless them mightily with a revelation of Your love. Bless them with prosperity, peace, joy, and love, in Jesus's name.*
>
> *In the name of Jesus, forgive me for allowing myself to grow bitter when Your Word commands me to forgive. I confess this sin and ask You to wash me clean. Remove all hints, traces, and residue of bitterness, unforgiveness, resentment, offense, strife, and discord from my heart. I reject and renounce wrong thoughts and feelings that try to rise up and remind me of the hurts and wounds of the past. Rip out every root associated with past pains.*

Help me, Lord, to recognize the enemy's strategy to trap me in resentment, bitterness, and unforgiveness. Help me not to hold people's sins against them. Teach me to avoid responding with a judgmental heart when I am hurting. Heal my emotions and renew a right spirit within me. In Jesus's name, amen.

CHAPTER 11

ABSALOM'S DISLOYAL AGENDA

DON'T MOURN FOR Absalom." I heard the Holy Spirit speak those words to my heart one day during intimate worship. This disloyal, rebellious spirit defiled one of our leaders at the Awakening House of Prayer, and I was forced to confront it or watch it destroy the ministry.

Admittedly I tolerated it for years. At first I didn't see it, though I'm convinced it was there all along like a dormant cancer waiting for a trigger to release deadly bullets. Many times spirits attached to God-loving Christians hide until they find an opportune time to strike. Other times it takes a trigger event to activate their operation. In other words, even someone carrying an Absalom can seem like the most loyal person you'd ever want to know—until he's not.

In our case, the Absalom leader was working to take over the ministry. It started after my itinerant ministry exploded. I was traveling to churches almost every week. I had a small team in place to run the prayer room, and everything seemed to be running smoothly. Trouble started arising when we launched the church expression one summer.

I had a specific vision from the Lord and wanted to

execute plans according to that vision. The Absalom consistently defied the vision. I started getting bad reports while traveling.

In one instance, I decided a woman who attended regularly should not be allowed to prophesy during services because she was bitter, hurt, and wounded. The prophecies she offered were often of a corrective nature over people in the ministry. What she was hearing was the Lord speaking to her about her own life, not the lives of others. So you can imagine my shock when I was on the road one week and received a call telling me this bitter woman was prophesying about me during a service while I wasn't there.

The Absalom leader was also preaching doctrine that was out of line with our beliefs as a ministry and began telling other leaders she did not have to honor the vision of the house because she'd been in ministry for many years. I was shocked and appalled. She had served with me loyally for a long season. But I could not ignore the reports, and if I was honest with myself, I had seen some of these haughty traits along the way but wanted to believe the best. After all, nobody is perfect.

After seeking advice from outsiders with more wisdom than I had, I realized I was dealing with an Absalom spirit. Immediately I put an end to the midweek Bible study while I prayed for a strategy to confront the issue. Absalom's response was to start another Bible study and openly hand out business cards to our regular attendees. Yes, this spirit was actually bold enough to do this right out in the open.

At that point I had to confront the situation head-on. I expected a fight, but this person left in peace. Soon, though, mutual friends called asking me why we would not return certain equipment. The individual was spreading lies about the ministry. Absalom's spouse started making repeated and ungodly threats against us, promising revenge. Suddenly we were having trouble with the city about issues in our building, issues the landlord had not fixed. We were soon forced to leave our location and roam about the city looking for a place to reestablish the house of prayer.

I learned firsthand that Absalom is a disloyal, rebellious spirit that defies leadership, builds alliances through common offenses, courts disgruntled people in order to form a coalition, misinterprets the gift of God and uses it for a wrong purpose, and otherwise wreaks havoc on the job site or home front, or in church.

ABSALOM'S ANGRY, OFFENDED HEART

Offense opens the door to many spirits. Just as the Absalom church leader took up an offense against me for standing in authority to execute the vision God gave me, the biblical Absalom certainly took up an offense against David for operating in his rightful authority as king. Ultimately pride and rebellion, along with a heart that does not trust leadership, are at the root of an Absalom spirit.

As the account in 2 Samuel 13 goes, Amnon, the son of David, fell in love with his half-sister Tamar. His friend Jonadab, David's nephew, gave him a strategy to woo Tamar to his bedroom and rape her. Absalom found Tamar immediately after the incident and took her into his care. David was angry but would not speak to Amnon pleasantly or angrily. He did not punish him in any way. "But Absalom hated Amnon because he had raped his sister Tamar" (2 Sam. 13:22). This event—and the way David dealt with it—created a wound in Absalom's heart and slowly turned him into a monster.

Absalom—a man who carried the traits that characterize

this spirit—waited two years to exact his revenge on Amnon. Two years later he ordered Amnon killed and then fled (vv. 28–34). Noteworthy is the fact that this spirit did not manifest again for another five years. Three years after Absalom fled, David forgave him and brought him back to Jerusalem, but Absalom did not see his father for two more years. Absalom was so angry over this royal snub that he ordered his servants to burn down Joab's field. When Absalom doesn't get what he wants from you, he'll start working to burn down what belongs to you, figuratively speaking.

Both Joab and David bowed to this angry, manipulative act. Joab told David what Absalom did to his field, and the king summoned his son. That's what Absalom was counting on. Absalom "bowed low to him, his face on the ground before the king; then the king kissed Absalom" (2 Sam. 14:33). David overlooked Absalom's crimes.

Just as there was no punishment for Amnon raping Tamar, there was no punishment for Absalom's murderous plot against Amnon. Perhaps David remembered having Uriah the Hittite murdered after he slept with his wife, Bathsheba, and could not bring himself to judge the matter. But just as spoiling our kids creates out-of-control teenagers, David's decision to treat Absalom's sins lightly created a monster.

Spiritual warriors, understand that the devil waits for an opportune time to strike (Luke 4:13). Just as we see with Absalom's behavior, someone can be in your family, your workplace, or your church and seem meek and mild for many years while carrying a spirit he picked up decades ago without even knowing it.

I remind you, we are not wrestling against flesh and blood (Eph. 6:12). One would think Absalom would be grateful David restored him to the kingdom, but instead he launched a conspiracy against his merciful father. This is why you cannot tolerate this spirit in your life. If you don't resist its operations at the onset, it will develop a strategy to dethrone you from your God-ordained position.

ABSALOM'S EVIL CONSPIRACIES

Once restored to the kingdom, Absalom wasted no time setting his wicked plans to overthrow David's kingdom into place. In 2 Samuel 15 we read about his strategy. He gathered a chariot, horses, and fifty men to run before him. He arose early in the morning and stood by the city gate, which was a seat of authority in Bible times.

> When any man who had a dispute concerning which he had come to the king for a judgment approached, Absalom would call to him and say, "Which city are you from?" And he would say, "Your servant is from one of the tribes of Israel." Then Absalom would say to him, "Look, your claim is good and right, but there is no one to hear you on behalf of the king." Absalom would continue, "If I were appointed a judge in the land, then every man who had a claim could come and I would give him justice." When a man would approach to bow before him, he would reach out, embrace him, and kiss him. Absalom acted this way toward every Israelite who came to the king for a judgment. So Absalom stole the hearts of the men of Israel.
>
> —2 Samuel 15:2–6

Absalom is a patient spirit. David's son did this for forty years, then asked his father to allow him to go fulfill a vow to the Lord in Hebron. The king permitted him to go, but Absalom had sent scouts to all the tribes of Israel with a clear instruction: "When you hear the sound of the horn, say: Absalom has become king in Hebron" (2 Sam. 15:10). Absalom gained immediate momentum with his coup. When David heard of it, the mighty man who had defeated so many of Israel's enemies fled.

That is the temptation that comes with this spirit's attack. You want to flee. You want to abandon the post the Lord set you in, whether in your home, your workplace, or your church. David left his house barefoot, his head covered and weeping. This is the man who slew the bear, the lion, Goliath, and many others in battle. As the women sang, "Saul has slain his thousands, and David his ten thousands" (1 Sam. 18:7).

In his wisdom, David sent some of his loyal followers back to Jerusalem to thwart Absalom's plans, but this was a passive response to an aggressive attack. He actually gave orders to deal with Absalom gently. You can and should deal with people gently, but you cannot deal with demons gently because demons certainly won't deal gently with you. Demons want to destroy you. Ultimately Joab took three spears in his hand and thrust them into Absalom's heart while he was caught by his hair in a tree. Joab's armor bearers killed him and sent a messenger to David with the news.

"The king was deeply moved and went up to the upper chamber of the gate and wept. As he went he said, 'O my son Absalom, my son, my son Absalom! If only I could have given my death in your stead, Absalom, my son, my son!'" (2 Sam. 18:33). Israel knew David was grieving for his son and were disgraced while David covered his face and cried, "My son Absalom, my son, my son!" You have to love David's heart, but his actions brought shame on Israel. Joab rebuked him for dishonoring those who stood with him against Absalom's coup (2 Sam. 19:5–7).

Even after Absalom's death there was fallout. It took David a little while to completely take back the kingdom. Unfortunately that's true when dealing with this spirit. After you defeat it, you will still have to clean up some messes. You will have to set some things in order that were out of order and opened the door to an attack. You will have to stay vigilant because Absalom has followers who may be planning a second coup.

ABSOLUTE SIGNS ABSALOM IS MANEUVERING AGAINST YOU

Absalom wants to rule the roost and uses tactics of division, secretiveness, and manipulation to accomplish its goal. It can manifest in a church, a workplace, or any setting where a leadership structure is established. A person operating in an Absalom spirit seeks to promote and exalt himself rather than waiting for God to exalt him. Absalom is all about self, self, and self.

This defies Scripture: 1 Peter 5:6 tells us to humble ourselves and God will exalt us at the right time; James 4:10 tells us to humble ourselves before the Lord and He will lift us up; and Jesus Himself warns that those who exalt themselves will be humbled and those who humble themselves will be exalted (Matt. 23:12). Know that Absalom will fall. It's just a matter of how much damage you permit this spirit to do before you send it packing.

Absalom is confident and self-assured by outward appearances. Second Samuel 14:25–26 tells us, "In all of Israel, there was no man as handsome as Absalom. From the sole of his foot to the top of his head, there was not a blemish on him. When he cut the hair of his head (and at the end of every year he cut it, for it was heavy on him), he weighed the hair from his head at two hundred shekels, according to the king's standard."

Those operating in an Absalom spirit are not necessarily physically attractive, but they will have some manner of charisma, talent, or charm that attracts people to them. They use that talent to find an open door and use that charm to steal the hearts of the people. It's difficult to uproot an Absalom spirit because people operating in this demonic force have labored to win friends and influence people through manipulation and by meeting their felt needs. Although a person tapping into an Absalom spirit seems confident on the outside, typically they are insecure, angry, and bitter on the inside—and usually they don't even know it.

Absalom wants to be seen and admired and will set up monuments for himself in your midst. A monument is something that honors a person. The Lincoln Memorial is a monument to Abraham Lincoln. Mount Rushmore in South Dakota is a monument to past presidents. North Carolina is home to a monument of Billy Graham. Typically people set up monuments for great men and women after they die. Second Samuel 18:18 tells us, "Now Absalom in his lifetime had taken and set up for himself a memorial stone in the Valley of the King, for he said, 'I have no son by whom my name may be remembered.' So he named the memorial stone after himself; and to this day, it is called the monument of Absalom."

Practically speaking, those operating in an Absalom spirit set up monuments with the words they speak. They boast on themselves. They remind you of how able they are—how much you need them. They talk about their great exploits from days gone by. They call attention to their gifts and talents. They point out their strengths. All of this is to convince you they are able to solve the problems you are facing and therefore are worthy of position. Remember, Absalom stood in the city gate and told all who came seeking justice how he could help them if he were only king. Absalom doesn't trust authority figures—and actually resents them based on a past hurt—and trusts himself more than God. (See 2 Samuel 13:20–21, when Absalom told his sister Tamar to stay at his house instead of going to their father after she had been raped. He did this because he trusted his way of dealing with the situation over anyone else's.)

Absalom operates with hidden agendas, secret strategies, and undercover alliances. Remember Absalom asked David to come to an event with sheepshearers. David declined, but Absalom urged him until he allowed his brother Amnon to go with him (2 Sam. 13:23–27). Amnon had raped his sister Tamar, and Absalom was readying to exact revenge. Absalom then commanded his servant to kill his brother. Later, we see two hundred men from Jerusalem going with Absalom as invited guests as he went to take the kingdom from his father, but the Bible says "unsuspecting; they did not know anything" (2 Sam. 15:11). Absalom gathers to itself unsuspecting followers who don't know they are part of a coup. Usually those whom Absalom draws also have bitter hearts.

Absalom is selfish and self-centered. Absalom manifests with self-interest, self-promotion, selfish ambition, self-advancement, and self-pity. This is an opportunistic spirit, always looking for a way to climb up the ladder until it reaches the top rung. Make no mistake: this spirit has insurrection in mind. As with any deception, people moving in this treacherous spirit usually do not see what they are doing. They may act religious and humble, but pride and rebellion are in the hearts of those under this demon's influence.

If you are dealing with this spirit in your midst, you have to confront it. It's similar to a Jezebel spirit, and it can be difficult to discern the difference. But the way to overcome it is similar: confront it. If the person will not repent, you must dismiss him or her from whatever group you are leading or cut personal ties because this spirit will steal your friends, turn your family against you, take your leadership position, and otherwise overrun your life if you let it. This political spirit recruits the people closest to you, as Absalom recruited Ahithophel, to strip you of your authority. (See 2 Samuel 16:15–23.) If you can't cut ties, pray long and strong and don't get into agreement with it.

ABOLISHING THE ABSALOM SPIRIT

The Absalom spirit is not something to take lightly. As you can see, it nearly ripped the kingdom out of David's hands. You must confront these atrocious operations in the spirit realm. Start with this prayer:

> *Father, in the name of Jesus, if I've sown seeds of rebellion or discord, forgive me. If there be any offense or resentment in my heart, deliver me. I repent of wrong attitudes and harmful mind-sets against leaders I've served in the past. I break any agreement with the Absalom spirit.*
>
> *Now, I stand in my authority against this wily spirit, and I command it to cease and desist its treacherous operations against my life. I command Absalom's conspiracy to fall to the ground. I decree and declare that none of Absalom's weapons against me shall prosper.*
>
> *Lord, expose Absalom's hidden agendas, secret strategies, and undercover alliances against me. I ask You to deliver those deceived by Absalom's charisma. Bring Absalom's insurrection to naught.*

Cancel the confederacy of wickedness against me. Give me the victory over my spiritual enemies and help me to discern this spirit if it counterattacks, in the name of Jesus. Amen.

CHAPTER 12

INFIRMITY'S INSIDE JOB

W HEN GLORIA MOVED into her new home, things seemed peaceful, but startlingly soon sickness and disease—an infernal demon of infirmity—unleashed a series of ferocious spiritual storms against her family. Gloria's husband, Jim, was diagnosed with cancer, and she was plagued with mysterious autoimmune disorders—and so was her dog.

Gloria and Jim valiantly warred against the cancer demons and the autoimmune hellions, but the victory was short-lived. Shortly after these victories, Jim landed in a wheelchair for the better part of a year, and Gloria began suffering erratic enemy strikes manifesting as severe nausea and headaches that came out of nowhere and for no apparent reason. Along the way Jim started having heart problems.

Mind you, these were healthy people who ate right, exercised, and otherwise took good care of themselves, body, soul, and spirit. They should have been walking in divine health, but instead they were riddled with sickness, disease, and pain. Much prayer and even deliverance went forth. After about a year of pondering and praying and peeling away at the onion, the root of the issue was discovered.

The Holy Spirit revealed a spirit of infirmity had taken up residence in their home under a former owner. This spirit would attack at opportune times—and it was never a convenient time. Although this Christian couple won battle after battle with the manifestations of the spirit's attacks, they never ultimately bound the strong man (Mark 3:27)—and they grew weary from the warfare. Gloria and Jim welcomed me and my intercessors to cast it out.

Since the spirit of infirmity was commanded to go, Gloria and Jim have not experienced any severe attacks on their health. Sure, they get colds like the average Joe, but the diseases and mystifying out-of-the-blue attacks have ceased. They are walking pictures of divine health, but they are not ignorant of this spirit's devices. They know all too well that the spirit of infirmity will come to strike again in due season. They are well armed and will war from a place of victory unto victory in the name of Jesus.

The spirit of infirmity works to defy your God-given promise of divine health (Isa. 53:4–5). This demon wants to keep your body weak and diseased so you cannot fulfill your destiny. Think about it for a minute. It's harder to walk in the Spirit, work in the flesh, or reason in your mind when you are severely ill. The serious sicknesses the spirit of infirmity wants to bring into your life will leave you in bed more than you want to be, missing work more than you can afford, and otherwise living in misery.

Although not every sickness is based in a spirit of infirmity, many serious illnesses are. We can open the door to the spirit of infirmity in our lives through any sin. However, some transgressions and mind-sets open the door wide to the spirit of infirmity. Issues like self-hatred and self-pity can cause our bodies to turn against itself. Sexual immorality also defiles our bodies (1 Cor. 6:18).

In general, disrespecting our bodies as the temple of the Holy Spirit (1 Cor. 6:19) can invite spirits of infirmity to attack. Denying the biblical reality of divine health and divine healing makes you an easy target because you won't fight back if doubt and unbelief deceived you. Fear can open the door to infirmity—in particular if you have a fear of getting sick. Depression is another open door because this spirit knows you don't have the strength to fight back. Bitterness, resentment, and unforgiveness offer the enemy gaping wide windows of opportunity to attack you with infirmity.

Specifically, in my experience bitterness sets the stage for cancer. That is why it's important to be quick to forgive (Col. 3:13). Colds and flus seem to attack people who are discouraged, overwhelmed, stressed, depressed, and hopeless. That's not to say that everyone who catches colds and flus in season carries these emotions. However, you may have noticed some people catch every bug that comes around. Even doctors will tell you stress and depression hinder your immune system. Cast your cares on the Lord because He cares for you (1 Pet. 5:7).

Any form of disobedience to God can open the door to the spirit of infirmity. Think about it. Adam and Eve's treason against God ultimately opened the door for sickness, disease, and death. Knowing this, we need to be quick to repent so we can slam these doors shut. If you find yourself in a battle with the spirit of infirmity, ask the Lord to show you the root. It could be a matter in your heart, or it could be, as it was with Gloria and Jim, a spirit of infirmity in your home or workplace that has established a stronghold.

A CLOSE-UP LOOK AT THIS SPIRIT'S OPERATION

In Luke's Gospel we find an account of a woman who had a spirit of infirmity for eighteen years—eighteen years! The

Bible tells us she was bent over and could not straighten herself up. Can you imagine? This story reveals the progressive nature of the spirit of infirmity. If you don't deal with it immediately as an outward attack, it will attach itself to you and begin overtaking you. The good news is, you can get immediate deliverance from this spirit.

When Jesus saw the woman with the spirit of infirmity,

> He called her and said to her, "Woman, you are loosed from your infirmity." Then He laid His hands on her, and immediately she was made straight and glorified God.
>
> —LUKE 13:12–13

The Greek word translated "infirmity" in this passage is *astheneia*. According to Strong's concordance it means "want of strength, weakness, infirmity." When it relates to the body, as it does in this context, it speaks of "its native weakness and frailty; feebleness of health or sickness."[1] Again, it's hard to accomplish God's will for your life if you are weak, frail, feeble, and sick.

We find this same spirit afflicting the woman with the issue of blood in Mark's Gospel. She suffered twelve years. Mark tells us she suffered "many things of many physicians, and had spent all that she had, and was nothing bettered, but rather grew worse" (Mark 5:26, KJV). When the doctors can't diagnose what's wrong with you—or when the diagnosis does not lead to a treatment that gets to the root of the health problem—there's likely a devil in the mix.

Again, I believe many diseases, including cancer, autoimmune issues, and arthritis, are demonic. Jesus, the Great Physician, did what many doctors could not do—He set the woman free. It was her desperate and persistent pursuit of the truth she believed with her heart and spoke with her mouth that pulled virtue from the hem of Christ's garment. He told her, "Your faith has made you well" (Mark 5:34).

It takes faith to battle the spirit of infirmity—but only a mustard seed's worth (Matt. 17:20). Sometimes you can seek deliverance ministry to find freedom. Other times you may have to walk it out on your own. Either way, doubt is an enemy to your healing and deliverance.

I remember many years ago I needed a healing—badly. I had several "medical conditions" in my physical body that manifested in a string of strange ways. The root of it was a whacked-out sympathetic nervous system that caused my heart to beat too fast and my blood pressure to rise to the point that I would become too dizzy to stand. I was taking medications for this "condition" for which there was no cure, and the medications, of course, caused more unwanted symptoms. I needed a healing.

When I got saved, someone told me God could heal people. They told me testimonies of seeing limbs grow out of stubs, blind eyes opening, and other miraculous works. They told me of healing ministers such as Benny Hinn and Oral Roberts. They told me healing is for today. I decided to give it a try. (That was my first mistake. You don't give God's Word your best shot. You give it your whole heart.)

I asked God to heal me. Nothing happened. I went to the church to have the elders lay hands on me. Nothing happened. I drove three hundred miles to attend a Benny Hinn crusade, determined to get my healing. Nothing happened. (Determination alone won't deliver results. You have to believe from your heart and speak with your mouth over and over again.)

I needed a healing, but all I wound up with was disappointment, and that disappointment led me into the death grips of doubt. The devil really had a heyday in my mind. He filled my head with all sorts of doubt—doubts about the truth of healing for today, doubts about God's ability to heal this rare "condition," even doubts about my own salvation. Once you entertain one doubt, you invite other "guests" such as uncertainty, misgivings, qualms, distrust, suspicion, skepticism, and, of course, unbelief.

You need to crash doubt's party with your faith and send it and its rascally friends home so you can see God move in your life. That's what I did, and today I am walking in divine health—and you can too.

THE BIBLE OPPOSES THE SPIRIT OF INFIRMITY

We know that Jesus went about doing good and healing all who were oppressed of the enemy (Acts 10:38). Jesus wants to heal you from the enemy's oppression. Decide to build up your faith to believe what He's already done for you. Let's look at some promises that will build your faith.

Prophesying about Jesus, Isaiah said, "Surely he has borne our grief and carried our sorrows; yet we esteemed him stricken, smitten of God, and afflicted. But he was wounded for our transgressions, he was bruised for our iniquities; the chastisement of our peace was upon him, and by his stripes we are healed" (Isa. 53:4–5).

Peter confirmed this promise in the New Testament as Jesus fulfilled the scripture—and continues to fulfill the scripture: "He Himself bore our sins in His own body on the tree, that we, being dead to sins, should live unto righteousness. 'By His wounds you were healed'" (1 Pet. 2:24).

The psalmist wrote, "Bless the LORD, O my soul, and all that is within me, bless His holy name. Bless the LORD, O my soul, and forget not all His benefits, who forgives all your iniquities, who heals all your diseases" (Ps. 103:1–3). Also, "He heals the broken in heart, and binds up their wounds" (Ps. 147:3). And, "I shall not die, but I shall live and declare the works of the LORD" (Ps. 118:17). Exodus 23:25 promises, "You shall serve the LORD your God, and He shall bless your bread and your water, and I will remove sickness from your midst."

Before you begin praying for your deliverance from the spirit of infirmity and the healing that follows suit, you need to get these and other scriptures down in your heart. Study who Jesus is. Of Himself, He declared:

> The Spirit of the Lord is upon Me, because He has anointed Me to preach the gospel to the poor; He has sent Me to heal the broken-hearted, to preach deliverance to the captives and recovery of sight to the blind, to set at liberty those who are oppressed.
>
> —LUKE 4:18

Meditate on Jesus as healer. Read the Gospel accounts of healing after healing and deliverance after deliverance. Listen to teaching CDs about healing, healing testimonies, and the like. Watch DVDs and YouTube videos with healing messages. Confess scriptures about healing out of your mouth. Decree and declare what the Word of God says about you and the promises that belong to you. It works.[2]

Again, if you've done something to open the door to the spirit of infirmity attacking you, you need to repent. Turn from the behavior or mind-set that is welcoming this wickedness into your physical body. Proverbs 3:7–8 says, "Do not be wise in your own eyes; fear the LORD and depart from evil. It will be health to your body, and strength to your bones."

Let your soul prosper by meditating on the Word day and night. Third John 2 reveals God's operations: "Beloved, I pray that all may go well with you and that you may be in good health, even as your soul is well." Many times our bodies are sick because our souls are sick.

Proverbs 4:20–22 says, "My son, attend to my words; incline your ear to my sayings. Do not let them depart from your eyes; keep them in the midst of your heart; for they are life to those who find them, and health to all their body."

If you can't break free on your own, humble yourself and ask for help: "Is anyone sick among you? Let him call for the elders of the church, and let them pray over him, anointing him with oil in the name of the Lord. And the prayer of faith will save the sick, and the Lord will raise him up. And if he has committed any sins, he will be forgiven" (James 5:14–15).

Let me say one last thing here: sometimes the root of infirmity is tied into liking the attention you get from being sick. Different from Munchausen syndrome, in which you are faking a sickness to get attention, in this case you may be sick but don't really want to get well because people are showing you favor, supporting your physical and emotional needs, and offering you their pity and prayers. I knew a woman who was constantly ill and although she told everyone not to tell anyone, everyone knew because she personally told all of them. If it wasn't back pain it was headaches, and if it wasn't headaches it was hormones causing her illness. The bottom line is, you have to want to get well or you will stay sick.

DON'T ANSWER INFIRMITY'S KNOCK ON YOUR DOOR

When you break free from the spirit of infirmity, know this with certainty: it will try to come back at an opportune time. In my experience, anything you break free of that carries a demonic nature will launch a new attack against you within the first several weeks of your newfound freedom. You have to stay especially vigilant in that time frame or the victory you celebrated will be short-lived.

When you are delivered from this particular spirit and healing comes to your body, false symptoms—or what the Bible calls "lying vanities"—will manifest sooner or later. Jonah 2:8 reveals, "They that observe lying vanities forsake their own mercy" (KJV). The word "lying" in that scripture essentially means an empty falsehood, according to Strong's concordance,[3] while the word "vanities" means vapor or breath.[4] These lying vanities are false witnesses against your healing. Proverbs 14:5 says "a false witness breathes lies" (NLT).

If the spirit of infirmity was causing pain in your body and you get free, for example, those symptoms of illness were a lying vanity. If your heart is healed and you feel the same symptoms come back a few months later, that's a lying vanity. This spirit wants you to accept its work. It wants to lie to your soul about what's going on in your body. It releases vain imaginations against your mind. Paul told us what to do in this instance:

> For though we walk in the flesh, we do not war according to the flesh. For the weapons of our warfare are not carnal, but mighty through God to the pulling down of strongholds, casting down imaginations and

every high thing that exalts itself against the knowledge of God, bringing every thought into captivity to the obedience of Christ, and being ready to punish all disobedience when your obedience is complete.

—2 CORINTHIANS 10:3–6

As with any other spirit, your battle with the spirit of infirmity is obviously not against flesh and blood. Therefore, you can't ultimately gain victory in battle against it with medicine and therapies. Whether you have been delivered from this wicked spirit or not, your battle is largely in the mind. You have to pull down the strongholds infirmity has erected or is trying to erect in your soul and cast down the imaginations hitting your mind. Infirmity's lies exalt themselves against the knowledge of God that declares you are healed. You have to bring those thoughts captive to the Word of God and keep standing and resisting until the lying vanities go.

When the devil comes knocking on your door with a package of infirmity, refuse to sign for it with the words of your mouth or the thoughts of your heart. Slam the door in infirmity's debilitating face and declare the healing that rightfully belongs to you by the blood of Jesus.

My testimony of healing is one example of how the devil sets us up. If you have been praying for the same thing for years and haven't received an answer, or if your track record for answered prayer is poor, it gets harder and harder to believe God wants to answer you the next time you pray. Seizing on your weakness, the devil will introduce doubtful disputations to your mind, and it becomes a vicious circle that only faith can break.

ERADICATING THE SPIRIT OF INFIRMITY

It's time to break the cycle of infirmity in your life—or learn how to break the cycle before it becomes a cycle. It is important that you understand as you pray this prayer that infirmity can come from a generational curse. With that in mind, let this prayer help you start breaking the spirit of infirmity off your life:

> *Father, in the name of Jesus I come to You with a heart full of forgiveness. I choose by my will to forgive those who hurt me, harmed me, maligned me, rejected me, cursed me, abused me, or used me. I forgive them now, and I ask You to forgive and bless them. Forgive me for harboring any resentment, bitterness, or unforgiveness in my heart.*
>
> *Lord, I repent for any and all disobedience and rebellion I've committed against You. Please show me any and all doors I have opened to let the spirit of infirmity or other spirits into my life. Forgive me for coming into agreement with demons and give me the grace to slam the door shut. I plead the blood of Jesus over myself, the blood that provides forgiveness and cleansing from all unrighteousness.*
>
> *I claim Psalm 103 and thank You for healing all my diseases. I claim Psalm 118:17, that I shall live and not die and will declare Your marvelous works. I claim Exodus 23:25s, that You take sickness away from my midst. I claim Isaiah 53:4–5, that by Christ's stripes I am healed and He carried infirmity far away from me. I break and bind the spirit of infirmity in my life right now, in Jesus's*

name. I submit myself to You, God. I resist infir-mity and command it to flee from me, in the name of Jesus. Amen.

CHAPTER 13

REJECTION'S ROTTEN RHYME AND REASON

REJECTION ONCE HAD a tight rein on my soul—and I didn't even know it. All I knew was I always felt like there was something wrong with me. I often felt like nobody really cared. I felt misunderstood most of the time. I often felt like people were talking about me behind my back. If I walked into a room or down the aisle in a store and people were laughing, I was sure they were laughing at me.

It was a miserable way to live—and it was unreasonable. On the home front, I had parents who loved me dearly and grandparents who adored me. In school I had good friends who believed in me and teachers who favored me. There was no natural reason I should feel so awkward and out of place in my own skin. But there was a spiritual reason—the spirit of rejection. As I look back, I have to wonder if seeds of rejection were planted in my preborn soul in the womb.

That spirit would go for the kill shortly after I got married to my college sweetheart. He was the photo editor and I was the managing editor of the school paper. We were quite the team. Instead of following my own passions, I helped him build his photography business—until I got pregnant with our daughter. At that point I decided to find a way to exercise my gifts, because I did not see myself as a stay-at-home mother.

I started pitching story ideas to magazines. Despite a rash of early rejection letters that fed my insecurities, I pressed on and found success in the world of journalism. By the time my daughter was twelve months old, I was managing editor of a huge website backed by two major names in media and managing a dozen writers daily. Although I didn't know the Lord, my gifts made room for me, and for the first time I gained great confidence.

Then it happened. My husband abandoned me with our then-two-year-old daughter. He moved to another country and started a new family, never to look back. The spirit of rejection that had been hovering over my life for decades saw an opportunity to completely crush me and began telling me lies that sounded like this: "Nobody will ever love you again. You'll die fat and alone. Nobody wants to be around you."

I started listening to those lies because I didn't know the truths I know now. I ate a box of doughnuts every day and gained fifty pounds within a few months. I started smoking like a chimney and sipping sweet liqueurs in coffee after my daughter went to bed at night. I stayed up all hours of the night rolling over in my mind what the enemy was telling me.

I felt worthless. I felt isolated because I believed no one could possibly understand how I felt—and I didn't yet know the Jesus who understands our pain and delivers us from our wounds. Thank God, He delivered me from that torment, and I am now able to show others the way to freedom from rejection's rotten rhyme and reason.

THE ROOTS OF REJECTION

Maybe you don't have a story of abandonment and betrayal to tell. Maybe you haven't experienced a traumatic event that causes you to feel rejected. I hadn't either—until I did. Nevertheless, that spirit chased me all the days of my childhood and teenage years. Consider that rejection could be speaking to you so subtly that you don't discern its voice or how it's shaping your life.

Remember when you were in elementary school and the kids chose teams on the playground? Someone was always picked last and felt rejected. Usually everyone knew who was going to get picked last, including the outlier. When you don't get that dream job you applied for, rejection is right there to attack. When the love of your life breaks up with you, rejection is ready to pounce. When your friends go to the movies without inviting you, rejection will rear its ugly head.

If your parents didn't come to your recitals in elementary school, it could have opened the door to rejection. If Mom favored your brothers and sisters over you, rejection may have entered your soul. If you didn't fit into the "in crowd" in high school, you probably faced rejection. If you've struggled with your weight, rejection probably spoke to your heart. If you didn't get into college or some other group you longed to align with, you probably felt the sting of rejection.

Sometimes rejection enters while a person is still in the womb. If your parents didn't want a child and felt you were a burden to them, if they were stressed out about another mouth to feed, if they wanted a girl and got a boy or vice versa, the spirit of rejection may have attacked you before you were born or at birth. The bottom line is that anytime you are rejected, the spirit of rejection is ready to pounce.

Whether rejection attacks your mind from the outside or has taken up residence in your soul, it's time to reject it. But we need to know its modus operandi before we can root it out.

Rejection works subtly to destroy your self-esteem and your purpose. Rejection causes you to feel sorry for yourself and play the victim. Rejection opens the door for other spirits, especially Jezebel, to build strongholds in your mind. Rejection spurs you to reject other people before they have an opportunity to reject you. Rejection wants you to base your worth on what you do instead of who you are in Christ.

It may shock you to learn that scientists liken the pain of rejection to physical pain. Researchers recruited forty people who had endured an unwelcomed romantic breakup to undergo an MRI brain scan. When researchers showed the subjects photos of their exes and asked them to think about being rejected, their brains lit up in the same area sensory pain activates. In a study published in the *Proceedings of the National Academy of Sciences*, researchers wrote, "These results give new meaning to the idea that social rejection 'hurts.'"[1] It also gives credence to the stronghold the spirit of rejection seeks to erect in the mind.

Indeed, psychologists have discovered that rejection does more than influence our emotions—it influences our cognition and physical health. Some rejected souls even become aggressive and turn violent. In a 2003 study of fifteen cases of school shooters, Mark Leary, a professor of psychology and neuroscience at Duke University, and his colleagues discovered that all but two of the shooters suffered from social rejection.[2]

Rejection is unreasonable. Guy Winch, PhD, a licensed psychologist and author of *Emotional First Aid: Healing Rejection, Guilt, Failure, and Other Everyday Hurts*, notes that rejection sends us on a mission to seek and destroy our self-esteem, temporarily lowers our IQ, and does not respond to reason.

"Participants were put through an experiment in which they were rejected by strangers," Winch wrote in an article about rejection. "The experiment was rigged—the 'strangers' were confederates of the researchers. Surprisingly, though, even being told that the 'strangers' who had 'rejected' them did not actually reject them did little to ease the emotional pain participants felt. Even being told that the strangers belonged to a group they despised such as the KKK did little to soothe people's hurt feelings."[3]

REJECTION IS AN ANCIENT ASSIGNMENT

If you feel rejected, you are not alone. Rejection is common to man. It's what you do with it that defines you. Think about it. Joseph's brothers rejected him, threw him into a pit, and sold him into slavery (Gen. 37). It wasn't because Joseph wasn't good enough; rather, it was because his brothers were jealous and felt threatened by his revelations. Joseph could have let his family's rejection destroy him. Instead, he worked through the hurt and his wisdom saved the world.

Leah faced mass rejection. Her father, her sister Rachel, and her husband Jacob dished out heaps of rejection on her soul. I can only imagine the pain she felt when she woke up next to Jacob after their wedding night and discovered he was shocked and dismayed to see her face instead of Rachel's. Jacob worked another seven years for Rachel and loved her more than Leah (Gen. 29:30). Leah at first tried to earn Jacob's love by bearing him children that then-barren Rachel could not offer, but she eventually learned to stop looking at man and keep her eyes on God (Gen. 29:35).

David experienced rejection upon rejection. When Samuel came to anoint one of Jesse's sons king, Jesse didn't think enough of David to call him in from the field (1 Sam. 16:11). When David brought food to his brothers at the battle line, they ridiculed him and accused him of having wrong motives. In 1 Samuel 17:28 we read that David's eldest brother, Eliab, asked him, "Why have you come down here? And with whom have you left those few sheep in the wilderness? I know your pride and the evil of your heart. For you have come down that you might see the battle."

Hagar felt the sting of rejection when Abraham sent her and her son Ishmael away (Gen. 21:8–21). Jeremiah's prophetic ministry was rejected over and over again. David faced rejection from Saul (1 Sam. 19), his wife Michal (2 Sam. 6:16, 20–23), the Philistine king who would not allow him to battle against Israel (1 Sam. 29), and at the hand of his son Absalom (2 Sam. 15). Of course, Jesus was rejected by His own family and His own kinsmen (Mark 6:1–6). Rejection is a reality of life. We must reject rejection—refuse to take it to heart. That can be easier said than done if you don't know who you are in Christ.

Now, there is true rejection, but there is also imagined rejection. Indeed, rejection often works through imaginations. The spirit of rejection can twist your perception of circumstances so it looks and feels as if you are being rejected even when you aren't. In the natural it's called a misunderstanding. But if you don't cast down the imaginations that ride on the back of misunderstandings, the spirit of rejection will work to form a stronghold in your mind that controls your thought patterns and makes it easy for this demon to hold you in bondage.

THE VOICE OF REJECTION

When I suffered from rejection—which was intertwined with shame, as the two often go hand in hand—I was sure people were talking about me when they weren't. I was convinced if I walked past a group of people who were laughing and one of them happened to make eye contact with me, they must be laughing at me. It's bad enough when you feel people are rejecting you. Satan's ultimate goal is to get you to reject yourself so you won't take care of your temple. Remember, infirmity can come in through self-rejection. When you are rejecting yourself, you're also sure God is not pleased with you.

I remember a time when I was really beating myself up over something. I was down on my knees virtually whipping myself with self-condemning pseudoprayers. I was just crying out to God over and over about the same weakness, asking Him to forgive me and wondering what was wrong with me.

There was nothing really wrong with me. I was just growing in character. But rejection was doing a number on me. And it didn't help that I had spiritual leaders who used shame as a tool to control the congregation.

Suddenly, in the midst of my self-rejection, I heard a still, small voice that said, "Would you just stop it?"

That startled me. After all, I was on my knees praying out of my heart to the Father. Why would He want me to stop?

When I stopped, the Holy Spirit said, "How would you like to watch your daughter sit there and beat herself up every morning?"

See, I wasn't praying. Not really. I wasn't approaching the throne of grace boldly to receive mercy and find grace in a time of need (Heb. 4:16). Not really. I was merely repeating to God the words rejection had recited to me as if they were gospel truth. I was condemning myself for an innocent matter of immaturity.

As I sat there silently, tears still rolling down my cheeks, the Holy Spirit said, "Go read Ephesians 1:6."

I have to admit, I didn't even know what that scripture said. Not exactly. I knew, generally speaking, that it had something to do with our redemption in Christ, but I wasn't sure what it said. I got off my sore knees and opened up my Bible. Wouldn't you know it? Ephesians 1:6 says, "He made us accepted in the Beloved" (NKJV).

Wow! That changed my whole perspective. God Himself interrupted my self-condemning prayer to let me know that He accepts me with all my faults and all my immaturities. From that point on I made it my mission to reject rejection and accept my God-given identity.

Whether you are in full-blown bondage to rejection or just have an occasional battle with this spirit, the remedy is the same: reject rejection and accept your God-given identity.

When I hear rejection begin to whisper that no one cares—and the spirit of rejection will often take the opportunity to say things like that when you are walking through a fiery trial—I tell that devil something like, "I cast all my cares upon the Lord, for He cares for me." (See 1 Peter 5:7.) And my punch line is always, "I am accepted in the Beloved."

REJECTING REJECTION GOD'S WAY

Chances are you'll have to reject rejection more than once, either on the home front, in the workplace, or among friends. Whether real or perceived, rejection doesn't just give up. If it can't turn you into a self-pity-toting performer, rejection will puff you up with pride to compensate for your insecurities.

Or it will lead you to fabricate a protective personality to guard yourself from more rejection. Rejection distorts your personality. The key to victory over rejection is to reject rejection in whatever form it takes and accept your God-given identity.

When rejection comes whispering to your soul, telling you that something is wrong with you—you aren't "this" enough, "that" enough, or "something else" enough—reject that thought in the name of Jesus. The truth is, you are fearfully and wonderfully made. You are complete in Him who is the head of all principality and power (Col. 2:10). You are God's workmanship, created in Christ for good works (Eph. 2:10). So reject rejection and accept your God-given identity.

Be conscious of your thoughts. Any thought with even the slightest hint of rejection should be immediately cast down and replaced with the truth. The truth is that God loves you (Rom. 8:37–39). The truth is that you were delivered from the power of darkness and translated into God's kingdom (Col. 1:13). The truth is that you are forgiven of all your sins and washed in the blood (Eph. 1:7). The truth is that you are the righteousness of God in Jesus Christ (2 Cor. 5:21). The truth is that you are submitted to God and rejection has to flee from you when you resist it (James 4:7). Get your Bible and take some time to circle or highlight every New Testament verse that says "in Christ." You'll discover who you are. Also study the love of God, which silences the voice of rejection.

I could go on and on and on. If you want to keep it really simple, do what I do. When rejection comes whispering, I tell that devil, "I am accepted in the Beloved." Nothing else matters. Not really. So reject rejection and accept your God-given identity in the name of Jesus!

ROOTING REJECTION OUT OF
YOUR LIFE FOR GOOD

Like fear, rejection is not a once-and-for-all battle, but you can root the spirit out of your soul for good if you reject rejection and guard your heart with all diligence. In other words, you may still hear the voice of rejection at times, but you can combat that by standing against it and embracing who you are in Christ. Use this prayer starter to root rejection out of your soul. You may have to pray this more than once:

> *Father, in the name of Jesus, I come to You boldly and with humility asking You to forgive me for heeding the voice of rejection when You have made Your great love abundantly clear. Renew a right spirit in me. I renounce and resist rejection and command it to go far from me in the name of the Lord. I command the voice of rejection to be silenced, and I take authority over all misperceptions, twisted lies of shame, and aggressive thoughts, in the name of Jesus.*
>
> *I break the power of shame, guilt, and condemnation that trail rejection. I refuse to reject myself any longer, because Your Word tells me I am accepted in the Beloved. I confess that You are my beloved and I am Yours. Therefore I slam the door shut on every notion of rejection that tries to enter my soul. I break the curse of generational rejection over my life and my family line. I stand against the fear of rejection. I cast rejection out of my soul in the mighty name of Jesus.*

Now, Father, fill me with Your Spirit, Your love, Your peace, and Your joy—and strengthen me to stand against this evil of rejection, in the name of Jesus. I forbid this spirit from operating in my soul ever again. Amen.

CHAPTER 14

JEALOUSY'S ENVIOUS EVIL

MY MOM OFFERED me plenty of cute Southern sayings and wise advice when I faced unpleasant circumstances growing up. When I was three years old, I used to see the spirit of fear in my bedroom, so Mom tucked me in with the phrase, "Night night, sleep tight. Don't let the bedbugs bite. Sweet dreams." I'm not sure how she expected me to have sweet dreams after she got me worrying about the bedbugs, but that's another story.

When I woke up in the morning, she would say, "Rise and shine, sleepy head." I suppose you would be sleepy too if you were battling bedbugs all night. When I got old enough to meet with persecution at the hands of my classmates, she always told me, "They're just jealous."

That saying was true. Jealousy and envy are a two-edged sword that breeds hostility and opens the door to all manner of wickedness. *Jealous*, according to Merriam-Webster's dictionary, means "hostile toward a rival or one believed to enjoy an advantage."[1] See, people can be jealous of what they think you have even if you don't have it—and even when they are not willing to put in the work to get it.

You may notice when you get a promotion or a breakthrough in the spirit, or when you receive a revelation from

God or a blessing, people around you wax jealous—but they are also envious. To be envious, Merriam-Webster's explains, is "feeling or showing a desire to have what someone else has." [2] In other words, they covet what you have, violating Scripture and robbing themselves of their own blessing.

In Exodus 20:17 the Lord commands, "You shall not covet your neighbor's house; you shall not covet your neighbor's wife, or his manservant, or his maidservant, or his ox, or his donkey, or anything that is your neighbor's." That's pretty clear, but consider this: being jealous and envious of what others have—being covetous—is on the list of cardinal sins with lying, stealing, adultery, and murder. Indeed, jealousy is a murderous spirit. It might not kill you in the natural, but it will certainly slander you in your community.

I've learned jealousy, envy, and slander work as a deadly trio to destroy your reputation and release witchcraft at your mind. You can read more about witchcraft in chapter 6. Jealousy is a work of the flesh (Gal. 5:19–21), but it can also be a spirit, and it wants to destroy. Saul was jealous of David and tried to kill him (1 Sam. 19). Joseph's brothers were jealous of him and tried to kill him (Gen. 37). Cain was jealous of Abel and did kill him (Gen. 4). People with a jealous spirit feel threatened. They feel overlooked. They feel like they deserve what God gave you—and they'll slander you in the name of Jesus to get it.

A GATEWAY TO ALL MANNER OF EVIL

Jealousy is a gateway spirit to evil. The Amplified Bible, Classic Edition really spells James 3:16 out: "For wherever there is jealousy (envy) and contention (rivalry and selfish ambition), there will also be confusion (unrest, disharmony, rebellion) and all sorts of evil and vile practices."

Jealousy breeds contention, and contention breeds confusion, unrest, disharmony, rebellion, and many other evil and vile practices. That makes jealousy a potent weapon in the hands of the enemy. The Bible actually says envy makes your bones rot (Prov. 14:30, NIV). You can't walk in love and walk in jealousy at the same time (1 Cor. 13:4). As Solomon said, "Wrath is cruel, and anger is outrageous, but who is able to stand before envy" (Prov. 27:4). Paul warns us not to envy one another (Gal. 5:26). And Peter warns us to put away all envy and slander (1 Pet. 2:1).

Jealousy and envy manifest from the Old Testament to the New. In modern days, jealousy rises up through a competitive spirit, petty comments, endless questions about what you are doing and who you are with, spying into your life by questioning your friends and family, looking through your phone or e-mail, eavesdropping on your conversations, trying to make you feel jealous, clinginess, and the constant need for reassurance.

Jealous and envious people may flatter you to your face but talk about you behind your back, remind you of your past mistakes, pick you to death with criticism, pretend to be happy for you but take subtle digs, embarrass you around your friends by telling old stories, or lash out and get angry at you for no apparent reason. Jealousy will ultimately lead them to murder your reputation through slander and divide you from the blessings of God. Let's consider just a few jealous and envious figures in the Bible:

Lucifer was jealous of God's power, leading to his rebellion.

We point out his pride, which is real, but the archangel also had selfish ambition rooted in jealousy. Isaiah 14:13–14 reveals, "For you have said in your heart, 'I will ascend into heaven, I will exalt my throne above the stars of God; I will sit also on the mount of the congregation, in the recesses of the north; I will ascend above the heights of the clouds, I will be like the Most High." Jealousy can lead to a great fall.

Leah and Rachel were jealous of each other.

Leah was jealous of Rachel because she was Jacob's favorite. Rachel was jealous of Leah because she bore Jacob children when she could not (Gen. 29–30). Strife rose up between them as they constantly contended for their husband's attention and affection. Their motives in bearing children became impure, and this jealousy left them—and Jacob—miserable much of the time. Jealousy corrupts your motives.

Miriam and Aaron were jealous of all the attention Moses was getting.

Moses was the leader of the Israelites and spoke face-to-face with God. His sister and brother started slandering him after he married a Cushite woman, saying, "Has the LORD spoken only by Moses? Has He not spoken by us also?" (Num. 12:2). That made God angry. Miriam became leprous as snow. Aaron escaped this wrath, which suggests that Miriam was the instigator. Aaron immediately repented. Jealousy in your heart makes the Lord angry.

Ahab coveted Naboth's vineyard.

In 1 Kings 21, King Ahab told Naboth to give him his vineyard because it was close to his house. He offered to pay Naboth for the plot or give him a better vineyard in exchange. Naboth told Ahab he could not oblige because the land was part of his inheritance. Ahab got mad and depressed. His wife, Jezebel, took matters into her own hands and had Naboth killed so Ahab could take his vineyard. Jealousy can turn murderous.

Haman was jealous of Mordecai.

In the Book of Esther we learn that Haman was second in command to King Ahasuerus of Persia. Mordecai would not bow to him because he was a Jew and didn't want to give Haman honor that belonged to God. When the king honored Mordecai in front of the nation, Haman devised a plot to have him and all Jewish people murdered. You know the story. Mordecai told Esther, who exposed Haman's plot. Haman was hanged on the gallows he prepared for Mordecai. Jealousy damages your own soul.

Martha was jealous of Mary's relationship with Jesus.

Martha was running around serving the King. Mary was sitting at His feet, enjoying His presence. Martha took note and grew jealous. Scripture says, "But Martha was distracted with much serving, and she came to Him and said, 'Lord, do You not care that my sister has left me to serve alone? Then tell her to help me.' Jesus answered her, 'Martha, Martha, you are anxious and troubled about many things. But one thing is needed. And Mary has chosen the good part, which shall not be taken from her'" (Luke 10:40–42). Jealousy causes attacks against others' character.

OBLITERATING THE SLANDEROUS SPIRIT OF JEALOUSY

Jealousy attacks through slander and does so at strategic times. To slander someone is "to make a false spoken statement that causes people to have a bad opinion of someone," according to Merriam-Webster's dictionary.[3] It means to defame, malign, vilify, and asperse, which are fancy words for a continued attack on someone's reputation.

In one week alone I was accused of having a Jezebel spirit, splitting churches, cussing out pastors, breaking and entering and stealing from churches, refusing to cooperate with pastors in my city for revival, and a few other choice things. It all stemmed from a jealous female pastor and a businessman who seemed to have an unrequited crush on me.

After that string of accusations I decided it was time to rejoice. I figured I was doing something right since Jesus said we would be hated and persecuted for His sake (John 15:18–25) just as He was hated and persecuted. And the more people spread ridiculous lies and rumors, the more I will lift up Jesus.

I take heart in this passage from the Sermon on the Mount: "Blessed are you when men revile you, and persecute you, and say all kinds of evil against you falsely for My sake. Rejoice and be very glad, because great is your reward in heaven, for in this manner they persecuted the prophets who were before you" (Matt. 5:11–12).

How we respond to mistreatment is one of the most important aspects of our spiritual lives. When we respond the right way, we climb higher—or go deeper—in the Spirit. In fact, a season of slander is a sure sign that we are up for a promotion.

By contrast, when we respond the wrong way, we get bitter. Over time that bitterness will defile our spirits and dull our ability to sense the presence of God or hear His voice. Bitterness is deadly—and it's easy for the people around you to discern. Where true humility lives, though, bitterness can't take up residence. But I'm getting ahead of myself.

As I said, I have endured plenty of mistreatment during

my life, and I can honestly say that I count it a blessing. By God's grace I've always managed to ultimately respond in meekness rather than retaliating against the poor soul manifesting the character of slanderous Satan. And I pray that God's grace will continue to pour over me as the slander continues from religious spirits, atheists, radical gay activists, and occasionally even those close to me.

DYING TO YOUR OWN REPUTATION

No one likes to be slandered. I don't enjoy it. It makes me sorrowful for the one who is committing the sin. The Bible says, "Whoever privately slanders his neighbor, him I will destroy" (Ps. 101:5). And Romans 1:30–32 suggests slanderers are worthy of death. Paul told us not to keep company with a believer who has "a foul tongue [railing, abusing, reviling, slandering]" (1 Cor. 5:11, AMPC). Scripture actually lists the slanderer among the sexually immoral, the covetous, idolaters, drunkards, and extortioners. The point is, God hates slander.

Understanding how seriously God takes slander has had a twofold impact on my heart. First, it makes me not want any part of slander. I don't want to engage in it, and I won't listen to anyone else engaging in it. If someone comes to me with slander on his lips, I put out the fire and bring gentle correction to help him avoid Satan's snare. Second, when I see the damage the slanderer is doing to himself by attacking me, I take pity on him. While he thinks his words are digging a pit for me, he is actually the one who is bound to fall headlong into the hole.

I've learned over the years to transfer my personal rights to God, knowing He will vindicate me amid the slander or any other mistreatment. And He has confirmed me time

and time again in the presence of my enemies when I give
Him the reins. As Paul wrote, "You were bought with a price.
Therefore glorify God in your body and in your spirit, which
are God's" (1 Cor. 6:20). I have committed my spirit into
the Lord's hands, and in return He takes responsibility for
my protection, provision, and vindication when necessary.

I don't want to be like the accuser of the brethren. And
I don't want to swap insult for insult (1 Pet. 3:9). I want
to be like Jesus, who, "when He was reviled, He did not
revile back; when He suffered, He did not threaten, but
He entrusted Himself to Him who judges righteously"
(1 Pet. 2:23).

God is the judge. He will make the wrong things right
in His way and in His timing. Vengeance is His. He will
repay (Rom. 12:19). I won't be overcome with evil, but I will
overcome evil with good (Rom. 12:21). I will rejoice when I
am persecuted because I know that when I respond the right
way, I am blessed. My first response is to pray for those who
persecute me. And pray. And pray. And pray some more. It
keeps my heart clean. I encourage you to do the same.

I've found it true, looking back over the many instances
when I have been mistreated, abandoned, robbed, persecuted, falsely accused, and otherwise slandered, that the initial sting of the mistreatment fades more quickly when I
walk in love, speak the truth in love without being defen-
sive, and refuse to retaliate. I've also found it true that God
repays, vindicates, and takes vengeance on my behalf. If you
respond with meekness in the face of mistreatment, you can
have the same testimony.

DON'T LET JEALOUSY DISTRACT YOU

Jealousy doesn't always attack through someone else. Jealousy can also rise up in our own hearts to distract us and cause us to attack others—and we've seen the biblical examples of the harm this can do to our souls. When jealous thoughts come your way, resist them in the name of Jesus. It's an attack against your blessing and your mission. Don't fall for it.

Even before the Holy Spirit fell on the believers on the Day of Pentecost, Christians in the early church refused to allow jealousy to distract them from their mission. After Judas betrayed the Lord and committed suicide, Peter pointed out Scripture stating that a new witness to Jesus's resurrection had to be appointed. Two men were proposed: "Joseph, called Barsabbas, who was surnamed Justus, and Matthias" (Acts 1:23).

> And they prayed and said, "You, O Lord, who know the hearts of all, show which of these two You have chosen to take part in this ministry and apostleship from which Judas by transgression fell, that he might go to his own place." And they cast their lots, and the lot fell on Matthias. And he was numbered with the eleven apostles.
>
> —Acts 1:24–26, nkjv

We don't see Justus getting jealous, making false accusations against Matthias, or throwing him in a deep well to die. Justus didn't pitch a hissy fit to the other disciples or seek to prove why he was better suited for the promotion. He didn't breed strife in the early church. In fact, the Bible says when the Day of Pentecost came, they were all with one accord in one place (Acts 2:1).

Justus didn't storm out of the Upper Room and spread rumors about the apostles. No, he went on to receive the Holy Spirit in the Pentecostal outpouring, and it appears he may have gone on to work with the apostle Paul and Mark, the cousin of Barnabas (Col. 4:10–11). Whether that's the same Justus or not, only the Lord knows. But somehow I believe Justus, of whom the disciples thought enough to select him as one of the two candidates to become an apostle, humbly went on to do great things for the kingdom of God. If you respond in humility when someone else gets the promotion you want, in time you'll get a promotion of your own. Remember jealousy's motives and don't fall for this two-sided attack—and by all means don't operate in this wicked spirit.

Cain was jealous of Abel. The Pharisees were jealous of Jesus. If you know these stories, you know jealousy never ends well.

If you are jealous or envious, ask the Lord what the root is. Often it is a lack of humility in your heart, or a lack of understanding that God is no respecter of persons and He will bless you as He has blessed others if you will walk in His Word.

Don't think less of yourself because someone else has something you want. Rejoice with those who rejoice. Greed can also drive jealousy into the heart of man, or it can produce a longing for recognition and promotion. All this is sin, whether it's in your heart or in the heart of someone you are dealing with.

The good news is, we can turn away from sin and rid ourselves of this Saul-like spirit.

COMBATING JEALOUSY'S ENVIOUS ATTACKS

If you walk in any measure of success—or even if people think you do—you will come toe to toe with jealousy. It will operate through people as a work of the flesh and as a spirit. The first step to taking authority over this wicked demon is to break agreement with jealousy in your own heart. Use this prayer as a starter to cast jealousy out of your presence.

Father, in the name of Jesus I come to You confessing any and all jealous or envious thoughts, feelings, words, or actions—known and unknown. I renounce all jealousy and envy—and other spirits they attract—even now and ask You to uproot it from my heart. Please cleanse me from this unrighteousness and forgive me for tapping into this evil.

Lord of hosts, I ask You now to remove from my midst every spirit of jealousy or envy and the evil they attract. Loose Your warring angels to battle against the spirits that are battling against me, including spirits of strife, slander, sabotage, murder, selfishness, competition, anger, and division. I come against these spirits in Your authority and ask You to banish them from my presence.

Lord, restore my reputation and credibility for Your Son's sake. Restore what the enemy stole in the natural. Silence the wagging tongues and bless those who curse me. I thank You that every tongue that rises up against me in judgment shall be shown to be wrong. Vindicate me, O Lord, from this murderous spirit and deliver the ones who have risen up against me from evil. Help them break free from jealousy and break into Your best life for them. In Jesus's name, amen.

CHAPTER 15

TRAUMA'S TERRORIZING VOICE

W<small>HEN</small> I <small>WAS</small> two years old, a family member locked me in a dark closet for hours. Although I cannot remember it (my parents told me the story), I'm quite sure that petrifying episode opened the door to a spirit of fear that plagued my life for decades, even well into adulthood. I believe a spirit of trauma also entered my young soul during my isolation in a cold, pitch-black imprisonment.

Trauma is "an emotional response to a terrible event like an accident, rape or natural disaster," according to the American Psychological Association (APA).[1] Shock and denial are among the emotions that often immediately follow the event. Longer term reactions can include "unpredictable emotions, flashbacks, strained relationships and even physical symptoms like headaches or nausea," the APA reports. "While these feelings are normal, some people have difficulty moving on with their lives."[2]

Trauma starts as a shock against the soul. Left unhealed, it attracts a demon that torments the person. The spirit of trauma wastes no time entering into minds, especially innocent young minds that are unable to process emotions like adults, but it can strike at any age. Adults who don't know how or refuse to take the trauma to the Lord are also subject to demonic oppression.

Keep in mind that trauma doesn't just open the door to other spirits such as fear, rejection, and self-hatred; it also opens the door for more trauma. In other words, trauma begets trauma.

Indeed, I experienced one trauma after another as a child, many times at the hand of one particular troubled family member. I broke my leg twice before I was eight and both times lay in a hospital bed in painful traction for weeks before my body was wrapped in a cast. I was bed-ridden for months and had to learn to walk all over again—twice. After such an ordeal, I was scared senseless my leg would break if it bore weight.

In high school, a boy who sat in my seat in the English class before mine blew his brains out when the bell rang, leaving my desk in a puddle of blood. A few years later someone came into my house brandishing a weapon and making bold threats against me. In other incidents, I stood watching as a police officer shot a man who was threatening to shoot him and literally sat two feet away from gangsters who had guns pointed at each other in a cocaine-induced standoff.

I've told you the traumatic story of my husband abandoning me with our two-year-old child. At another time, a police officer beat me black and blue and I was arrested for a crime I didn't commit. I landed in jail for forty days with hard-core drug dealers, prostitutes, and violent criminals. One woman in my dorm got "jumped" in the middle of the night and was sorely beaten. Therefore I slept only when the lights were on during the day, and only for a few hours. I was vindicated from the false arrest, but I was traumatized. As I shared in chapter 10, I found Jesus in that jail cell, and in time He healed me from the trauma and all the spirits that entered in with it.

Despite the inner healing movement, which has done a lot of good for a lot of people, many Christians experience traumatic events and never seem to find healing. When a reaction is unreasonable, it's usually a spirit at work. People won't hear reason because trauma's terrifying voice is speaking loud and clear, keeping them from moving past their past.

RECOGNIZING TRAUMA'S CONSTANT ATTACKS

You could be carrying a spirit of trauma and not even know it. It's possible you experienced a traumatic event your memory has blocked out because it's too painful to process. You can even experience trauma in your mother's womb. If you feel something is wrong but can't put a finger on it, you may be experiencing one of trauma's attacks.

Although we don't want to go navel-gazing—searching for problems we may or may not have—the Holy Spirit is faithful to bring up issues when He knows we are strong enough to face them. Trauma leaves clear markers of its work in your life. Here is a list of emotional, psychological, and physical symptoms associated with trauma, as listed in HelpGuide.org:[3]

- Shock, denial, or disbelief
- Confusion, difficulty concentrating
- Anger, irritability, mood swings
- Anxiety and fear
- Guilt, shame, self-blame

- Withdrawing from others
- Feeling sad or hopeless
- Feeling disconnected or numb
- Insomnia or nightmares
- Fatigue
- Being startled easily
- Racing heartbeat
- Edginess and agitation
- Aches and pains
- Muscle tension

"Symptoms typically last from a few days to a few months, gradually fading as you process the unsettling event," the report reads. "But even when you're feeling better, you may be troubled from time to time by painful memories or emotions—especially in response to triggers such as an anniversary of the event or something that reminds you of the trauma."[4] If you are still experiencing a number of these symptoms and you are otherwise healthy, a spirit of trauma could be terrorizing you.

The sooner we take our issues—any issues—to Jesus, the Healer, the easier it will be to wade through the recovery process. Think of it like a burn, which is essentially trauma to your skin. What you do in the first five minutes is vital because the heat from the burn is not isolated. In other words, the heat continues damaging tissue even after the heat source is removed. So the faster you move to cool the burn, the less damage it ultimately does to your skin and the more quickly you can recover.

Although there is a natural process of grieving and healing in the emotional realm, the faster you run to Jesus, the less damage trauma will ultimately do to your soul. The sooner you let Him in with His healing balm of Gilead, the better off you will be. Scripturally speaking, consider Paul's command: "Do not let the sun go down on your anger" (Eph. 4:26). It is dangerous to hold on to and meditate on toxic emotions. The sun may go down on your trauma, but you can choose to turn to the Lord immediately and ask Him for the grace to heal instead of wallowing in a victim mind-set.

THE ENEMY'S PLANS FOR TRAUMA

The unfortunate reality is that trauma is part of life. Every person who walks the face of the earth will experience some kind of trauma at some point. It's traumatic when a loved one dies. Divorce, near-death experiences, bad car accidents, sexual abuse, a horrific health diagnosis, school shootings, abandonment, engaging in war, getting robbed, miscarrying a baby, having an abortion, watching your home burn down, living through a natural disaster, getting fired from a job, or being rejected in social situations can open you up to trauma's bondage.

We see plenty of trauma in the pages of the Bible. Adam and Eve's son was murdered at the hand of his brother (Gen. 4). Moses, the great deliverer of the children of Israel, died suddenly before entering the Promised Land, leaving the Israelites reeling (Deut. 34). Jacob's daughter Dinah was raped, one of several disturbing cases of rape we see in Scripture (Gen. 34). Rachel wept for her lost children (Jer. 31:15). David returned to Ziklag to find it burned down and the enemy having taken captive his wives and children and those of his men (1 Sam. 30).

Many of us go through trauma and tragedy in our lives. When we do, we have two choices: submit our broken souls to the Holy Spirit so He can pour out the healing balm of Gilead, or harden our hearts, choose unforgiveness, and invite demons to erect strongholds in our minds. Whether it's a divorce, spiritual abuse, death, or even post-traumatic stress disorder, God can breathe on your soul and restore your mind. You can recover from life's traumatic trials.

There are many practical steps you can take to walk through trauma. You may need help from your pastor or a counselor experienced in working with trauma survivors. Although you can cast out the spirit of trauma, unless you heal the damaged emotions the initial impact caused, you will get only a measure of relief and may wind up seven times worse than you were before the deliverance. This is true of any deliverance, but it is especially true of issues with high emotional impact. Consider Christ's words:

> When an unclean spirit goes out of a man, it passes through dry places seeking rest, but finds none. Then it says, "I will return to my house from which I came." And when it comes, it finds it empty, swept, and put in order. Then it goes and brings with itself seven other spirits more evil than itself, and they enter and dwell there. And the last state of that man is worse than the first.
>
> —MATTHEW 12:43–45

We need to process and work through emotions associated with trauma, such as anger, shame, survivor guilt, grief, fear, depression, and trust issues. We need to face the past and determine to move past it. We must learn to see the Lord as our protector and vindicator—our refuge. We also must learn to identify triggers that bring back old thoughts and feelings, and work through those thoughts and feelings as they arise. We must cast down imaginations and choose to think on things that are pure, lovely, and of a good report without denying our feelings. Again, you may need help with this. The battle really is in the mind.

We need to understand who we are in Christ and who He is in us to reject trauma's lies. When we meditate on the Word, it builds faith in our hearts, renews our minds, restores hope in our souls, and gives us confidence to move on with God. It allows us to truly exchange trauma for triumph. We move from feeling like victims to victors. We learn to receive His comfort and ultimately everything that comes with His Spirit—namely, true and lasting liberty from trauma. Indeed, trauma's veil—that veil that skews reality—is removed. It is as the apostle Paul wrote:

> Nevertheless when anyone turns to the Lord, the veil is removed. Now the Lord is the Spirit. And where the Spirit of the Lord is, there is liberty. But we all, seeing the glory of the Lord with unveiled faces, as in a mirror, are being transformed into the same image from glory to glory by the Spirit of the Lord.
> —2 CORINTHIANS 3:16–18

No matter what has happened to you, your identity is secure in Christ. Beyond studying verses about the love of God, which are abundant, you can meditate on these ten scriptures to overcome trauma and gain lasting victory:

1. "Therefore, if any man is in Christ, he is a new creature. Old things have passed

away. Look, all things have become new"
(2 Cor. 5:17).

2. "For we are His workmanship, created in
Christ Jesus for good works, which God prepared beforehand, so that we should walk in
them" (Eph. 2:10).

3. "There is therefore now no condemnation for
those who are in Christ Jesus, who walk not
according to the flesh, but according to the
Spirit" (Rom. 8:1).

4. "God made Him who knew no sin to be sin
for us, that we might become the righteousness of God in Him" (2 Cor. 5:21).

5. "You are of God, little children, and have
overcome them, because He who is in you
is greater than he who is in the world"
(1 John 4:4).

6. "But you are a chosen race, a royal priesthood,
a holy nation, a people for God's own possession, so that you may declare the goodness of
Him who has called you out of darkness into
His marvelous light. In times past, you were
not a people, but now you are the people of
God. You had not received mercy, but now
you have received mercy" (1 Pet. 2:9–10).

7. "I will praise you, for You made me with fear
and wonder; marvelous are Your works, and
You know me completely" (Ps. 139:14).

8. "But God, being rich in mercy, because of His
great love with which He loved us, even when

we were dead in sins, made us alive together
with Christ (by grace you have been saved),
and He raised us up and seated us together
in the heavenly places in Christ Jesus, so that
in the coming ages He might show the surpassing riches of His grace in kindness toward
us in Christ Jesus" (Eph. 2:4–7).

9. "I am confident of this very thing, that He
who began a good work in you will perfect it
until the day of Jesus Christ" (Phil. 1:6).

10. "I can do all things because of Christ who
strengthens me" (Phil. 4:13).

You truly can do all things through Christ. He is your
Rock, your Fortress, and your Deliverer (Ps. 18:2). Your
latter really will be greater than your past (Hag. 2:9). God
will give you beauty for ashes, the oil of joy for mourning,
and the garment of praise for the spirit of heaviness (Isa.
61:3). As He did for Job, God in His restorative power can
give you double for your trouble (Job 42:10). As one who
experienced trauma upon trauma, I'm a living testimony.

A PRAYER TO STRIP TRAUMA
OF ITS POWER

To strip trauma of its power, you need to start by forgiving
the person or people who caused the trauma, releasing God
from any responsibility, and perhaps forgiving yourself. Once
you've done that, you can pray this prayer. Your Counselor
and Comforter, the Holy Spirit, will help you pray.

*Father, I come to You in the name of Jesus and ask
You to heal my emotions from the spiritual attacks*

and natural circumstances that caused me such great pain. Release me from the painful memories of my past that continue to haunt my soul. Help me to think on what is lovely, pure, holy, and good, and to cast down imaginations that work to draw me away from Your presence and into a prison in my mind.

I give You my pain. I give You my fear. I give You my guilt. I give You my anger. I give You my anxiety. I give You every emotion that defies Your lordship and ask You to give me joy, peace, and strength in my spirit.

Deliver me from the nightmare and bondage caused by the trauma. Rescue me from the terrifying pit of panic attacks. Undo the damage the enemy did to my soul. Help me to slam the door on trauma once and for all. I plead the blood of Jesus over my mind, will, and emotions. Thank You for Your healing power working in me right now. In Jesus's name, amen.

PART FOUR

THE POWER TO OVERCOME

CHAPTER 16

DIFFERENTIATING BETWEEN DEMONS AND EMOTIONS

THE LIST OF demons that could attack a believer is long. You may be battling with depression and anxiety right now. You may carry a spirit of abandonment from a broken marriage or a lost parent. Barrenness may be attacking your spiritual or physical womb. Bondages of many kinds can manifest in your life, and the roots of many are found in this book.

But sometimes it's not a demon. Sometimes your spiritual warfare battle plan must include blowing up the enemy's vain imaginations coming against your mind, will, and emotions. Watchman Nee once said the believer's worst enemy is his emotions. I believe that. I've experienced it, and I've seen others fall prey to the enemy through the emotional realm.

The bottom line is, you can do spiritual warfare all day and all night. You can call the elders to lay hands on you and cast out devils. You can fast and read your Bible. But if you don't win the battle in your mind, if you don't submit your emotions to the Word of God, you could allow the devil entrance to kill, steal, and destroy.

Your thought life is powerful. The Bible says as a man thinks in his heart, so is he (Prov. 23:7). Your thoughts become words and your words drive you to action. Legally we have the mind of Christ, yet the Bible tells us to be transformed by the renewing of our minds (Rom. 12:2). When we renew our minds, it strengthens us to do the Father's will and stabilizes our emotions. Toxic emotions will produce a toxic life without any help from the wicked one. We must live out these verses:

> For though we walk in the flesh, we do not war according to the flesh. For the weapons of our warfare are not carnal, but mighty through God to the pulling down of strongholds, casting down imaginations and every high thing that exalts itself against the knowledge of God, bringing every thought into captivity to the obedience of Christ, and being ready to punish all disobedience when your obedience is complete.
>
> —2 CORINTHIANS 10:3–6

Our minds are full of imaginations. Holy imaginations are good. Imagining God's plans and purposes is wise. But imaginations of past hurts, fearful events, and the like must be cast down—and cast down quickly. We will not maintain victory over the enemy when we do not obey the warfare strategy in Scripture to stop meditating on negative thoughts that lead us out of God's peace.

YOUR REAL WORST ENEMY IS CLOSER THAN YOU THINK

"Give me the reins." I'll always remember when the Holy Spirit spoke those four words to my heart. It was clear He wasn't asking for one "rein"; He wanted all my "reins."

Of course, I immediately thought of a horse's reins. The

rider uses the reins as a restraining influence to control the animal with his or her guiding power. That example coupled with Scripture offered me insight into what the Holy Spirit meant and delivered me into a new level of freedom in Christ. When David invited Jehovah to "Examine me, O LORD, and prove me; try my reins and my heart" (Ps. 26:2, KJV), he was speaking of his emotions. The Hebrew word translated "reins" in this verse means "seat of emotion and affection."[1]

David, the man who asked one thing from the Lord—to dwell in His house all the days of his life and to gaze on His beauty and seek Him in His temple (Ps. 27:4)—was confident in who he was in God. Despite the warfare, despite the betrayal, despite the rejection—despite everything—David submitted his emotions to God.

We are all emotional beings. God gave us emotions—and God Himself has emotions. Think about it for a minute. Sometimes we feel joyful; sometimes we grieve. Sometimes we feel bold; sometimes intimidated. Sometimes we feel triumphant; sometimes completely and utterly physically and emotionally exhausted.

Our emotions can be a great motivator at times and a great enemy at other times. In fact, Watchman Nee, author of such books as *Spiritual Discernment*, *Secrets to Spiritual Power*, and *Let Us Pray*, once said emotions are the believer's number-one enemy—not the devil, but our emotions. That is why we need to give God our reins.

If we give God the reins of our hearts, we will find stability—but we have to give Him all the reins or we will be in danger of pulling in the wrong direction as we run our races. If we pick and choose which emotions we will submit to God and which ones we'll allow free rein in our souls, we will wind up unstable—and wound up. We'll find ourselves holding on tight as the emotional roller coaster turns us upside down and leaves us spinning in circles.

We need to align our emotions with the Word of God. Yes, I know. That's easier said than done. But if David did it, so can we. It's not a matter of putting on a soldier's face and keeping a stiff upper lip. David poured out his emotions to God—the anger, the disappointments, the hurt, the confusion—but he didn't wallow in those emotions. He submitted them to the One who could stabilize his soul.

GIVE GOD THE REINS

God gave us a free will, and it takes an act of our will to consistently submit our emotions to God. Job had to submit his emotions to God in the midst of a trial that caused his wife to encourage him to curse God and die (Job 2:9). Though his "reins be consumed within" him, Job had to decide to trust God despite facing a trial like few of us will ever see (Job 19:27, KJV).

God tries the hearts and reins (Ps. 7:9, KJV) not because He doesn't know how mature we are but so we can see how mature we are—or aren't. God knows when we are saying the right things out of our mouths but our hearts are actually far from Him (Jer. 12:2). God knows when we are suppressing emotions that lead to resentment, unforgiveness, and bitterness. He wants us to give Him the reins.

Yes, there is a time to weep and a time to laugh, a time to mourn and a time to dance, a time to love and a time to hate, as Solomon shares in Ecclesiastes 3. But it's always time to rejoice in the Lord—not in our circumstances but in the Lord. I believe choosing to rejoice in Him as an act of our will is one of the most strategic ways to submit our emotions to Him—to give Him the reins of our hearts.

A soulish life is dangerous, but if we give God the reins of our hearts, we will mature and be able to use our emotions to glorify Him rather than allowing them to lead us away from our purpose in Him. David put it this way: "I will bless the LORD, who hath given me counsel; my reins also instruct me in the night seasons. I have set the LORD always before me: because he is at my right hand, I shall not be moved" (Ps. 16:7–8, KJV).

GETTING OFF THE EMOTIONAL ROLLER COASTER

Is it possible that we could avoid the extreme highs and lows of the emotional roller coaster if we maintained God's perspective? What if we could wait on the Lord, mount up with wings as eagles, and take a prophetic perspective of our lives, and then rejoice in the Lord for the victory?

Paul the Apostle had a Holy Ghost–knack for putting things into perspective, which I believe gave him stability in his calling despite natural emotions that could have derailed him—and all too often derail others, if only for a few hours. When we see Paul react emotionally in Scripture, it is usually out of concern for others, save perhaps his frustration over John Mark that caused his split from Barnabas early in his ministry (Acts 15:36–41).

Paul wasn't "in his feelings" for himself. But he wasn't emotionless either. The emotions he displayed were rather selfless. If he was grieved, it was because someone was hurting. If he was weeping, it was because souls were being lost.

Yes, Paul displayed a righteous indignation toward sin. Yes, he exposed some by name who needed to be exposed. But his motive was always to advance and protect the kingdom of God despite any personal cost and without any personal agenda. When we can take that perspective, we can do great things for God—and indeed we will do great things for God.

Here is a perfect example of how Paul put things into perspective: After Paul was imprisoned, he discerned that not all gospel preachers had pure motives. In fact, he realized some were preaching Christ as a personal jab to him, even as he sat in chains while writing to the Philippians. In Paul's own words:

> Some indeed are preaching Christ out of envy and strife, and some also from good will. The former preach Christ out of contention, not sincerely, intending to add trouble to my circumstance. But the latter preach out of love, knowing that I am appointed for the defense of the gospel. What then? Only that in every way, whether in pretense or in truth, Christ is preached. And in this I rejoice. Indeed, I will rejoice.
> —Philippians 1:15–18

PAUL DIDN'T GET IN A TIZZY

For a while I was living in the Book of Philippians, and those verses continued to strike me. Paul could have put himself in a tizzy, calling out false apostles who were motivated by selfish ambition and who were actively working to breed strife. He could have allowed deep frustration to set in as he continued to hear about these preachers with impure motives who were freely roaming the streets while he was standing waist-deep in sewage in defense of the gospel. But Paul took a different perspective—and that perspective kept him emotionally stable.

Paul had his mind set on things above, not on the things of this earth. He thought on things that were true, noble, pure, lovely, and of a good report, things with virtue and praiseworthiness. He told us to think on such things in Philippians 4:8 because he knew from personal experience the power of doing so. Instead of grumbling and complaining about false apostles he could do nothing about, Paul found something about which to rejoice: even if they did have bad motives, those false apostles were proclaiming Christ's name every time they opened their mouths. The only thing that ultimately mattered to Paul was that Christ's name was preached, whether he was doing it or his enemies were doing it. In that he rejoiced.

There were also times when Paul was grieved. When Epaphroditus, his brother and fellow soldier, almost died working with him in the ministry, Paul grieved (Phil. 2:25–30). And we know that Paul wept over those who set themselves up as enemies of the cross of Christ, whose end is destruction, whose god is their belly and whose glory is in their shame—who set their mind on earthly things (Phil. 3:17–19). Yet Paul had a different perspective. Paul ultimately maintained a posture of rejoicing.

THE FELLOWSHIP OF CHRIST'S SUFFERINGS

Paul experienced the fellowship of Christ's sufferings more than most of us ever will. But he was stable in his calling despite the emotions that surely tried to invade his soul. We talk about our tests and trials. Well, three times Paul was beaten with rods, once he was stoned, three times he was shipwrecked, and a night and a day he spent in the deep (2 Cor. 11:25).

We talk about how the devil is attacking us. On Paul's journeys he was in danger from rivers and robbers, as well as Jews and Gentiles. He was in danger in the city, in the wilderness, on the sea, and among false believers.

We talk about our burnout for the kingdom. Paul labored hard, had many sleepless nights, and was often without food and exposed to cold weather. All the while, he was burdened for the church (2 Cor. 11). I realize all of our problems are relative, but Paul faced much worse than most of us ever will—and he nevertheless rejoiced. The good news is, so can we! It's a decision.

To be sure, I believe the key to Paul's emotional stability was his decision to rejoice in the Lord. No matter which way Paul's emotions were trying to sway him, he remained constant and fearless in the face of his enemies. Paul refused to give in to ungodly emotions that would lead him away from his purpose even for a few hours. Paul consistently rejoiced, through the good and the bad.

The concept of rejoicing or joy appears sixteen times in Paul's letter to the Philippians, which, again, was written from a jail cell. Paul discussed joy in suffering, joy in serving, joy in believing, and joy in giving. The joy of the Lord is our strength, friends.

What if we adopted a lifestyle of rejoicing? I'm not talking about rejoicing for the trial, but rejoicing in it. What if we rejoiced with those who rejoiced rather than being jealous killjoys? What if we decided by our will that no matter which way our emotions wanted to take us, we could do as Paul did and find something in the situation to rejoice about? What if…?

DEALING WITH HURT FEELINGS

Before we move on, it's important to discuss hurt feelings. This is the inroad to so much demonic activity in our lives. When we find our emotions stinging because of something said or done to us, we need to submit our emotions to the

Lord immediately for healing. Ironically much of the hurt we face comes at the hands of other believers—especially in the church.

So what do you do? First, pray. It may be that the Lord is going to deal with the person directly and anything you say would just make matters worse. But pray and see if the Lord can give you a graceful way to explain how you feel. It's important that you don't make accusations against those who hurt you. Use language such as "When you did this, I felt like this..." or, "When you say this, I feel like that."

Many times people don't even realize they've hurt us and would be quick to apologize if they did. But remember, love covers. It is not always necessary to go to those who hurt us every time they do something we don't like. It could be that the Lord is working something out in us. Maybe we're too sensitive. We always need to check our hearts. Is the person really being hurtful, or are we looking at the situation through filters of past hurts, rejection, or anger that cloud the truth? Ask the Lord.

Whatever the Lord shows you about the specific situation, ultimately you must forgive those who hurt you. As I mentioned previously, forgiveness is not for the other person— it's for you. Forgiveness doesn't justify what someone did that was wrong, nor does it necessarily mean that the relationship goes right back to where it was. If you don't forgive, you end up bitter and resentful, and before too long you'll end up hurting other people—and coming under the influence of a wicked spirit.

Jesus gave us the Golden Rule in the Sermon on the Mount: treat others the way you would have them treat you. We're all super busy these days, and most people want more from pastors and their brothers and sisters in Christ than they can possibly offer. We need to walk in love to the best of our ability and be sensitive to the Holy Spirit. If we sense that there has been an offense, we should be proactive about reaching out to correct it.

Some hurts are imaginary and some hurts are real. Either way, we must release them to God in order to be free from the pain. Consider these words the Holy Spirit spoke to my heart:

> When the feeling of hurt arises, the spirit of offense comes on the scene to fortify the pain, tempting you to hold on to the grudge in your heart. Therefore the proper response to emotional pain of the soul is always an immediate confession of forgiveness from the heart. The alternative to forgiveness from the heart is the ongoing torment of the soul. So if you want to be free from your hurts and wounds, take thoughts of forgiveness, meditate on them, and confess them rather than taking thoughts of the hurt. This is God's way—and it's the only way that brings true healing. And while you are at it, pray for those who have hurt you. This process will cleanse your heart and renew your mind. And you will walk free from the pain of your past.

Amen? Don't let your emotions get the best of you. Submit them to the Word of God and run to Him when you feel hurt, betrayed, overlooked, misunderstood, judged, or any other emotion that moves you from the position of peace and joy Jesus died to give you.

CHAPTER 17

WAGING WAR THAT WINS

EITHER THE DEVIL isn't fleeing or one demon is lined up right after the other to take the last one's place—at least that is the thought that crosses my mind in seasons of heavy spiritual warfare. I'm resisting the devil all right, but it sure doesn't seem as though he's fleeing—much less fleeing seven ways, according to the promise of Deuteronomy 28:7.

Despite the fact that I resist with all my might, sometimes the enemy continues raging against me like he's deaf or oblivious to the power in the name of Jesus. Yet I know God is not a man that He should lie (Num. 23:19). The Word is absolutely, 100 percent true all the time, without fail. And God's Word says every knee must bow to the name of Jesus (Phil. 2:10). So what gives?

When God's Word doesn't seem to be working, this I know: it's not God's Word that isn't working. Usually we're either missing some revelation or doing something wrong somewhere, whether we realize it or not. Either way, we need a revelation!

That is why I've penned this book. Its pages unmask the strategies and operations of the spirits that most frequently combat believers in our generation. Although there are many other demons that could plague you not listed in these pages, I believe you're well on your way to conquering hidden enemies in your life at this point. Learning to discern the many spirits revealed in this book will sharpen your spiritual senses to see other spirits operating.

This book is full of solid spiritual food, and Hebrews 5:14 says, "But solid food belongs to those who are mature, for those who through practice have powers of discernment that are trained to distinguish good from evil." I believe you have received both practical equipping and spiritual impartation through this book, as I've prayed for all those who read its pages to grow in discernment, wisdom, and effective prayer.

With that in mind, let's look at this "resist the devil" scripture in context as we explore principles on waging war that wins. The Bible actually says:

> But He gives more grace. For this reason it says: "God resists the proud, but gives grace to the humble." Therefore submit yourselves to God. Resist the devil, and he will flee from you. Draw near to God, and He will draw near to you. Cleanse your hands, you sinners, and purify your hearts, you double-minded.
> —JAMES 4:6–8

Isn't that a far cry from what you hear in some spiritual warfare circles?

WHO'S RESISTING WHOM?

First of all, the Greek word translated "resist" in James 4:7 is *anthistémi*, which means to "take a complete stand against" or a "contrary position" and "refusing to be moved."[1] Well, we can't take a complete stand against an enemy with whom we are standing in some measure of agreement. When you keep this passage of Scripture in context, it offers a clue about why the devil may not flee: we aren't fully submitted to God. That is why it's a good idea to repent and glorify God before engaging the enemy. That's why every prayer in this book contains an element of repentance. You should always repent before engaging in warfare.

We may be walking in pride that is causing God to resist us even while we're trying to resist the devil. Indeed, we can actually take pride in our spiritual warfare skills—and many do. I came out of a spiritual warfare camp some years ago that was especially proud of its fierce spiritual soldiers. We considered ourselves the Navy Seals of spiritual warfare. Yet the devil rarely fled. It seemed like there was never any lasting breakthrough. Even David had seasons of rest from war (2 Sam. 7:1).

Again, pride in our spiritual warfare skills can cause us to stumble before our enemies, because God resists the proud and gives grace to the humble. We need the grace of God to overcome our enemies. Flaunting our spiritual warfare skills like a boastful five-star general will most certainly lead to some measure of defeat eventually.

King Ahab, Jezebel's husband and a mighty warrior who posted many victories, was certainly full of pride. God's prophet Micaiah clearly told him what no false prophet on the king's payroll dared: that he would lose if he went to battle in Ramoth Gilead (1 Kings 22:1–23). Instead of heeding the voice of God's prophet, proud Ahab arrested the man of God and ran to the battle line anyway. He was killed in battle.

JESUS IS NOT A MAGIC WORD

We also can't overcome the enemy if we think we can toss around the name of Jesus like it's a magic word. True and lasting victory comes through not only faith in the name of Jesus but also intimate relationship with Him. You can't have consistent warfare-winning faith in a God you don't really know, because when the pressure is on, you need to truly believe He has your back. Knowing Jesus as your warrior and submitting to Him as your king each play a role in equipping you to send the devil packing.

Remember the itinerant Jewish exorcists who took it upon themselves to use the name of Jesus to cast out demons? They proclaimed, "We command you to come out in the name of Jesus whom Paul preaches" (Acts 19:13). No intimacy there. Seven sons of a Jewish chief priest named Sceva took that approach and experienced disastrous results (vv. 11–20). The devil didn't feel threatened at all: "The evil spirit answered, 'I know Jesus, and I know Paul, but who are you?' Then the man in whom the evil spirit was jumped on them, overpowered them, and prevailed against them, so that they fled from that house naked and wounded" (vv. 15–16). How embarrassing!

See, these Jewish exorcists didn't have a relationship with Jesus, so they really didn't have faith in His name. They had faith in Paul's ability to use His name, but you can't cast out devils in the authority of your pastor. God has given us victory in warfare, but we need faith firmly rooted in Him before we can truly stand in our authority in Christ and enforce that victory in the face of our enemies.

Of course, there can be other reasons the devil doesn't flee. I don't have all the answers—not by a long shot. Sometimes I really do think there's just an onslaught of demons that come one after another. You command one to flee, and there's another right there to take its place. Even if I don't know all the reasons we don't always seem to prevail during seasons of attack, I do know this: if we worship God in the midst of the battle, He will war against our enemies. So while we shouldn't hesitate to go on the offensive against our enemies with revelation from the Holy Spirit, I believe worshipping God generates the intimacy with His heart, the faith in His name, and the humility we need to remain victorious in warfare no matter how many devils come rushing our way.

BREAKING THE POWER OF VICIOUS CIRCLES

Have you ever found yourself in spiritual battle and it felt as if you were living in a vicious circle? You're trying your best to solve a problem, but every step you take seems to be making the problem worse—or even creating new problems.

If you can relate, stop and ask yourself, is this a vicious circle or a demonic cycle? In other words, is one trouble in your life leading to another because of the classic law of cause and effect, a law that can easily snowball for better or worse? Or are you wrestling against principalities and powers, against the rulers of the darkness of this world, against spiritual wickedness in high places (Eph. 6:12)?

Before we go on, let me state emphatically that not every obstacle or setback we face in life is rooted in demonic activity. Becoming super-skilled in spiritual warfare isn't going to solve all of your problems, because not all of your problems originate with demons. Getting hyperfocused on identifying demons and tearing down strongholds can actually perpetuate the vicious circle. What we magnify tends to manifest. Magnify the devil and he will seem bigger in your eyes. Magnify Jesus and His glory will inspire you to overcome by His grace.

With all that said, demonic cycles—a phrase I use to describe how demons create and manipulate strongholds in our minds to tempt us to walk around the same mountain over and over again—are real. Demonic cycles are more than just bad habits—and they can be more difficult to break, because you may not even recognize there is a mental stronghold involved in your drama. And you can't break the power of something you don't know is there.

Demonic cycles could manifest as overeating, job instability, yearly sickness, relationship issues, problems with authority, and many other undesirable woes. Demons can whisper in your ear and fortify ungodly thoughts in any area of your mind that isn't renewed. In this way, the demonic cycle may actually empower the vicious circle.

With demonic cycles, spirits often work to perpetuate acts of self-sabotage of which you are unaware. You start a new job but have the same personality conflict with the boss that you encountered at the last job. You get a new boyfriend and soon enough end up having the same arguments you had with the last boyfriend. You plan to get up an hour earlier to read your Bible and pray but you end up getting distracted by less-than-eternal purposes. So you find yourself looking for a new job and a new boyfriend even as you are dying on the vine because you aren't feeding your spirit. The common denominator is you. Whether you know it or not, you are allowing a demonic cycle to continue. Are you beginning to see it?

Breaking the power of vicious circles is often a matter of making better choices, but when it's a demonic cycle you need to identify the imaginations and wrong thought patterns that are allowing wicked spirits to wreak havoc on your life. Ultimately you have to take responsibility for your choices. No demon in hell is stronger than a will aligned with the Word of God. God's grace floods the soul that seeks first the kingdom of God and His righteousness.

The apostle Paul offers some good advice: "For though we walk in the flesh, we do not war according to the flesh. For the weapons of our warfare are not carnal, but mighty through God to the pulling down of strongholds, casting down imaginations and every high thing that exalts itself against the knowledge of God, bringing every thought into captivity to the obedience of Christ, and being ready to punish all disobedience when your obedience is complete" (2 Cor. 10:3–6).

In order to break demonic cycles rooted in soulish strongholds, you have to make a purposeful and diligent effort to cast down the imaginations that defy the Word of God. As believers we have the privilege of using God's Word to tear down barriers erected against His truth. We have the power to fit every loose thought, emotion, and impulse into the structure of a life shaped by Christ. Our tools are ready at hand for clearing the ground of every obstruction and building lives of obedience into maturity.

Beloved, that's good news! If you want to break demonic cycles in your life, humble yourself and ask the Holy Spirit to help you find the scriptures that will serve as your double-edged sword to slice into pieces the demonic strongholds in your mind. Even if it's a generational curse or you need full-blown deliverance, the blood of Jesus, the name of Christ, and the Word of God are more powerful weapons than anything Satan has in his arsenal.

Dig down to the root of your thinking. Where did it start? Forgive anyone who hurt you. Forgive yourself. Receive forgiveness from the Lord for your wrong thinking and self-sabotage. Ask the Lord to fill you with His Holy Spirit, love the people around you, take on a new attitude, and call those things that be not as though they were (Rom. 4:17). As you do, you will begin to see things as He does—through the eyes of faith—and your behavior will begin to change. You will break the demonic cycle and stop walking in vicious circles. I assure you, whom the Son sets free is free indeed (John 8:36).

SEVEN WAYS TO MAKE THE DEVIL FLEE

When you are living in covenant with God, you can stand on the blessings of Deuteronomy 28. One of them deals specifically with spiritual warfare: "The LORD will cause your enemies who rise up against you to be defeated before you; they will come out against you one way and flee before you seven ways" (Deut. 28:7).

See, God has promised us that He will cause our enemies who rise against us to be defeated before our faces. He declared that they shall come out against us one way and flee before us seven ways. But we can get in the way of our blessing and leave room for the enemy to stand in our faces rather than fleeing seven ways. With that in mind, here are seven tactics to make the devil flee seven ways.

1. Diligently obey the voice of the Lord your God.

In order to see the promise of Deuteronomy 28:7 come to pass in your life, you need to understand it in context. Deuteronomy 28:1 clearly states, "Now it will be, if you will diligently obey the voice of the LORD your God, being careful to do all His commandments which I am commanding you today..." This is your foundation. God doesn't expect us to be perfect. We cannot keep the law. That's why Jesus came to pay the price of our sin. But we should be seeking perfect obedience. We should diligently listen to God's voice and obey what He tells us by His Spirit and in His Word. This alone would cause many devils to run for the hills.

2. Repent before you engage in battle.

We have all sinned and fallen short of the glory of God (Rom. 3:23). There are sins of commission and sins of omission. Many of us think wrong thoughts, say wrong words, or take wrong actions over the course of the day. That means we are not fully obeying the voice of the Lord our God. When that's the case, we need to repent so we aren't standing on common ground with the enemy. It's difficult to defeat an enemy that already has you in a corner. Repent for any known sin and run to the battle line!

3. Know that God is on your side.

In Exodus 15:3, the children of Israel knew where they stood and where God stood. After the great deliverance from Egypt, they declared in song, "The LORD is a man of war; the LORD is His name." They knew that "the LORD shall go forth like a mighty man; He shall stir up zeal like a man of war. He shall cry out, yes, raise a war cry; He shall prevail against His enemies" (Isa. 42:13). They knew the battle belonged to the Lord (1 Sam. 17:47). They understood that they were God's battle-ax and weapons of war (Jer. 51:20).

4. War from a position of victory.

When Goliath challenged the army of Israel, the soldiers were scared witless of the Philistine champion. But David was a covenant man and understood that victory belonged to him in God. As believers we war from a position of victory, knowing that God always leads us in triumph in Christ (2 Cor. 2:14). We are more than conquerors through Him who loved us (Rom. 8:37). And if God is for us, then who can be against us (v. 31)?

5. Praise your way through.

In the Song of Moses in Exodus 15, the children of Israel sang a song to the Lord that went something like this: "The LORD is my strength and song, and He has become my salvation. He is my God, and I will praise Him; my father's God, and I will exalt Him" (v. 2). Of course, that was after Israel's deliverance from Egypt. If you want to make the devil flee, praise God before you engage in battle. Praise brought down the walls at Jericho (Josh. 6), and praise gave Jehoshaphat victory in battle: "When they began singing and praising, the LORD set ambushes against Ammon, Moab, and Mount Seir, who had come against Judah; so they were defeated" (2 Chron. 20:22).

6. Take up your armor.

We all know God has given us His armor, as outlined in Ephesians 6. But how many of us actually put it on before running to the battle line? Get a revelation of the belt of truth, the breastplate of righteousness, the shoes of peace, the shield of faith, the helmet of salvation, and the sword of the Spirit. Take some time to understand what this really means as part of your covenant with God. Satan cannot defeat the obedient soldier of God who is armored up and ready to fight. He will likely flee toward someone who is undressed, unrepentant, or uninformed about our covenant.

7. Pray always and be watchful.

At least half the battle is being on the offensive—and that demands discernment. There is an oft-overlooked instruction in Ephesians 6 that allows your spiritual warfare to transcend space and time: "praying always with all prayer and supplication in the Spirit, being watchful to this end with all perseverance and supplication for all the saints"

(Eph. 6:18, NKJV). The enemy is less likely to pounce on the one who is prayerful and watchful, because that person is in communion with the Holy Spirit, a power no foe can withstand.

So go forth, spiritual warrior, with praise in your heart and prayer on your lips, dressed for battle. The battle belongs to the Lord, and the devil will flee seven ways. He has no choice when you submit yourself to God and resist him.

NOTES

INTRODUCTION

1. James Strong, *The New Strong's Expanded Exhaustive Concordance of the Bible* (Nashville: Thomas Nelson, 2001), s.v. *"archē,"* accessed April 17, 2017, https://www.blueletterbible.org/lang /Lexicon/Lexicon.cfm?strongs=G746&t=KJV.

2. W. E. Vine, *Vine's Expository Dictionary of New Testament Words,* Volume 2 (Zeeland, MI: Reformed Church Publications, 2015), s.v. *"archē."*

3. Strong's Concordance, s.v. *"exousia,"* accessed April 17, 2017, https://www.blueletterbible.org/lang/Lexicon/Lexicon.cfm ?strongs=G1849&t=KJV; Strong's Concordance, s.v. *"exousia,"* accessed June 8, 2017, http://biblehub.com/greek/1849.htm.

4. Ibid., s.v. *"ponēria,"* accessed April 17, 2017, https://www.blue letterbible.org/lang/Lexicon/Lexicon.fm?strongs=G4189&t=KJV.

5. *Merriam-Webster Online,* s.v. "malice," accessed April 17, 2017, https://www.merriam-webster.com/dictionary/malice.

6. Strong's Concordance, s.v. *"kosmokratōr,"* accessed April 17, 2017, https://www.blueletterbible.org/lang/Lexicon/Lexicon.cfm ?strongs=G2888&t=KJV.

7. Ibid., s.v. *"skotos,"* accessed April 17, 2017, https://www.blue letterbible.org/lang/Lexicon/Lexicon.fm?strongs=G4655&t=KJV.

CHAPTER 1
ANTICHRIST SPIRITS' ANTI-ANOINTING AGENDA

1. Strong's Concordance, s.v. *"antichristos,"* accessed April 17, 2017, https://www.blueletterbible.org/lang/Lexicon/Lexicon.cfm ?strongs=G500&t=KJV.

2. Ibid., s.v. *"Christos,"* accessed April 17, 2017, https://www.blue letterbible.org/lang/Lexicon/lexicon.cfm?strongs=G5547&t=KJV.

3. Chuck D. Pierce and Rebecca Wagner Sytsema, *The Future War of the Church* (Ventura, CA: Regal, 2007).

4. Ibid.

5. Nash Jenkins, "Hundreds Gather for Unveiling of Satanic Statue in Detroit," *Time*, July 27, 2015, accessed June 7, 2017, http://time.com/3972713/detroit-satanic-statue-baphomet/.

6. Sarah Pulliam Bailey, "In the First Majority-Muslim U.S. City, Residents Tense About Its Future," *Washington Post*, November 21, 2015, accessed June 7, 2017, https://www.washingtonpost.com/national/for-the-first-majority-muslim-us-city-residents-tense-about-its-future/2015/11/21/45d0ea96-8a24-11e5-be39-0034bb576eee_story.html?utm_term=.f94feb0dafd7; International Mission Board, "Detroit-Warren-Dearborn, MI Metro Area," PeopleGroups.info, accessed June 7, 2017, https://www.peoplegroups.info/site/MetroHighlight/id/19820/name/Detroit-Warren-Dearborn.

7. "The Ten Most Dangerous U.S. Cities," *Forbes*, accessed June 7, 2017, http://www.forbes.com/pictures/mlj45jggj/1-detroit/.

8. "Flint Water Crisis Fast Facts," CNN.com, last updated April 10, 2017, accessed June 7, 2017, http://www.cnn.com/2016/03/04/us/flint-water-crisis-fast-facts/.

9. Donald James, "HIV Crisis in Detroit," *Michigan Chronicle*, accessed June 7, 2017, http://michronicleonline.om/2014/06/18/hiv-crisis-in-detroit/; Beth Dalbey, "Record-High STD Rates in US: Where Metro Detroit Ranks," *Detroit Patch*, October 21, 2016, accessed June 7, 2017, https://patch.com/michigan/detroit/record-high-std-rates-us-where-metro-detroit-ranks.

10. David Wilkerson, "Falling Away to the Antichrist!" World Challenge Pulpit Series, June 26, 1995, accessed June 7, 2017, http://www.tscpulpitseries.org/english/1990s/ts950626.html.

CHAPTER 3
LEVIATHAN'S TWISTED LIES

1. Strong's Concordance, s.v. "*livyathan*," April 18, 2017, https://www.blueletterbible.org/lang/Lexicon/Lexicon.cfm?strongs=H3882&t=KJV.

2. Ibid.

3. David L. Cooper, "Rules of Interpretation, Part 3" Biblical Research Monthly 1947, 1949, accessed June 7, 2017, http://www.biblicalresearch.info/page49.html.

4. Strong's Concordance, s.v. *"bariyach,"* accessed April 18, 2017, https://www.blueletterbible.org/lang/Lexicon/Lexicon.cfm ?strongs=H1281&t=KJV.

CHAPTER 4
PYTHON'S PERILOUS SQUEEZE

1. Collins English Dictionary, s.v. "estrapade," accessed May 22, 2017, https://www.collinsdictionary.com/us/dictionary/english /estrapade.

2. Jentezen Franklin, *The Spirit of Python* (Lake Mary, FL: Charisma House, 2013), 3.

3. Ibid., 6.

4. Strong's Concordance, s.v. *"pythōn,"* accessed April 19, 2017, https://www.blueletterbible.org/lang/Lexicon/Lexicon.cfm ?strongs=G4436&t=KJV.

5. Vine's Expository Dictionary, s.v. *"pythōn,"* accessed April 19, 2017, https://www.blueletterbible.org/lang/Lexicon/Lexicon .cfm?strongs=G4436&t=KJV.

6. Bible Gateway, "About the Darby Translation," accessed April 19, 2017, https://www.biblegateway.com/versions/Darby -Translation-Bible/.

7. Erik Ortiz and Rebecca Davis, "Snake Hunters Descend on Florida Everglades for Python-Killing Challenge," NBC News, February 14, 2016, accessed June 8, 2017, http://www.nbcnews .com/news/us-news/snake-hunters-descend-florida-everglades -python-killing-challenge-n517741.

8. Jessie Szalay, "Python Facts," Live Science, February 19, 2016, accessed April 19, 2017, http://www.livescience.com/53785 -python-facts.html.

9. Ibid.

10. Ibid.

11. Bryan Walsh, "Invaders: How Burmese Pythons Are Devouring the Everglades," Time, January 31, 2012, accessed June 8, 2017, http://science.time.com/2012/01/31/invaders-how-burmese -pythons-are-devouring-the-everglades/.

CHAPTER 5
RELIGION'S UNRIGHTEOUS RULES

1. Strong's Concordance, s.v. "*ouai*," accessed April 19, 2017, https://www.blueletterbible.org/lang/Lexicon/Lexicon.cfm?strongs=G3759&t=KJV.

2. *Merriam-Webster Online*, s.v. "woe," accessed April 18, 2017, https://www.merriam-webster.com/dictionary/woe.

3. Ibid., s.v. "hypocrite," accessed April 19, 2017, https://www.merriam-webster.com/dictionary/hypocrite.

4. Strong's Concordance, s.v. "*typhlos*," accessed April 19, 2017, https://www.blueletterbible.org/lang/Lexicon/Lexicon.cfm?strongs=G5185&t=KJV.

5. Ibid., s.v. "*hodēgos*," accessed April 19, 2017, https://www.blueletterbible.org/lang/Lexicon/Lexicon.cfm?strongs=G3595&t=KJV.

6. Ibid., s.v. "*mōros*," accessed April 19, 2017, https://www.blueletterbible.org/lang/Lexicon/Lexicon.fm?strongs=G3474&t=KJV.

7. Ibid., s.v. "*harpagē*," accessed April 19, 2017, https://www.blueletterbible.org/lang/Lexicon/Lexicon.cfm?strongs=G724&t=KJV.

8. Ibid., s.v. "*anomia*," accessed April 19, 2017, https://www.blueletterbible.org/lang/Lexicon/Lexicon.cfm?strongs=G458&t=KJV.

CHAPTER 6
WITCHCRAFT'S WICKED POWER

1. Strong's Concordance, s.v. "*qecem*," accessed April 20, 2017, https://www.blueletterbible.org/lang/Lexicon/Lexicon.cfm?strongs=H7081&t=KJV.

2. *Merriam-Webster Online*, s.v. "witchcraft," accessed April 20, 2017, https://www.merriam-webster.com/dictionary/witchcraft.

3. Strong's Concordance, s.v. "*kesheph*," accessed April 20, 2017, https://www.blueletterbible.org/lang/Lexicon/Lexicon.cfm?strongs=H3785&t=KJV.

4. Ibid., s.v. "*kashaph*," accessed April 20, 2017, https://www.blueletterbible.org/lang/Lexicon/lexicon.cfm?strongs=H3784&t=KJV.

5. Ibid., s.v. *"pharmakeia,"* accessed April 20, 2017, https://www
   .blueletterbible.org/lang/Lexicon/Lexicon.cfm?strongs
   =G5331&t=KJV.

6. Gesenius' Hebrew-Chaldee Lexicon, s.v. *"kesheph,"* accessed
   April 20, 2017, https://www.blueletterbible.org/lang/Lexicon
   /Lexicon.cfm?strongs=H3785&t=KJV.

7. For more about overcoming spiritual attacks of various kinds,
   see Ryan LeStrange, *Overcoming Spiritual Attack* (Lake Mary,
   FL: Charisma House, 2016).

CHAPTER 7
DEATH'S DANGEROUS STING

1. *Merriam-Webster Online*, s.v. "grief," accessed April 20, 2017,
   https://www.merriam-webster.com/dictionary/grief.

CHAPTER 9
JUDAS'S BETRAYING BLUEPRINTS

1. *Merriam-Webster Online*, s.v. "betray," specifically "Definition of
   Betray for English Language Learners," accessed April 21, 2017,
   https://www.merriam-webster.com/dictionary/betray.

2. *Merriam-Webster Online*, s.v. "Judas," accessed April 21, 2017,
   https://www.merriam-webster.com/dictionary/Judas.

3. Ibid.

CHAPTER 10
THE BAIT OF BITTERNESS

1. *Merriam-Webster Online*, s.v. "resentment," accessed April 21,
   2017, https://www.merriam-webster.com/dictionary/resentment.

2. Ibid., s.v. "bitter," accessed April 21, 2017, https://www
   .merriam-webster.com/dictionary/bitterness.

3. Ibid., s.v. "forgive," specifically "Definition of Forgive for English Language Learners," accessed April 21, 2017, https://www
   .merriam-webster.com/dictionary/forgive.

4. Strong's Concordance, s.v. *"pikria,"* accessed June 8, 2017,
   https://www.blueletterbible.org/lang/Lexicon/Lexicon.cfm
   ?strongs=G4088&t=KJV.

CHAPTER 12
INFIRMITY'S INSIDE JOB

1. Strong's Concordance, s.v. *"astheneia,"* accessed April 22, 2017, https://www.blueletterbible.org/lang/Lexicon/Lexicon.cfm?strongs=G769&t=KJV.

2. For a helpful resource, see John Eckhardt's *Prayers That Bring Healing* (Lake Mary, FL: Charisma House, 2010).

3. Strong's Concordance, s.v. *"shav',"* accessed April 22, 2017, https://www.blueletterbible.org/lang/Lexicon/Lexicon.cfm?strongs=H7723&t=KJV.

4. Ibid., s.v. *"hebel,"* accessed April 22, 2017, https://www.blueletterbible.org/lang/Lexicon/Lexicon.fm?strongs=H1892&t=KJV.

CHAPTER 13
REJECTION'S ROTTEN RHYME AND REASON

1. Ethan Kross et al., "Social Rejection Shares Somatosensory Representations with Physical Pain," *Proceedings of the National Academy of Sciences* 108, no. 15 (April 12, 2011): 6270, http://www.pnas.org/content/108/15/6270.full.pdf.

2. Kirsten Weir, "The Pain of Social Rejection," *American Psychological Association* 43, no. 4 (April 2012): 50, accessed April 23, 2017, http://www.apa.org/monitor/2012/04/rejection.aspx.

3. Guy Winch, "Ten Surprising Facts About Rejection," Psychology Today, July 3, 2013, accessed April 23, 2017, https://www.psychologytoday.com/blog/the-squeaky-wheel/201307/10-surprising-facts-about-rejection.

CHAPTER 14
JEALOUSY'S ENVIOUS EVIL

1. *Merriam-Webster Online*, s.v. "jealous," accessed April 23, 2017, https://www.merriam-webster.com/dictionary/jealous.

2. Ibid., s.v. "envious," specifically "Definition of Envious for English Language Learners," accessed April 23, 2017, https://www.merriam-webster.com/dictionary/envious.

3. Ibid., s.v. "slander," specifically "Definition of Slander for English Language Learners," accessed April 23, 2017, https://www.merriam-webster.com/dictionary/slander.

CHAPTER 15
TRAUMA'S TERRORIZING VOICE

1. "Trauma," American Psychological Association, accessed April 24, 2017, http://www.apa.org/topics/trauma/index.aspx.
2. Ibid.
3. "Emotional and Psychological Trauma: Healing from Trauma and Moving On," HelpGuide.org, accessed April 24, 2017, https://www.helpguide.org/articles/ptsd-trauma/emotional-and -psychological-trauma.htm.
4. Ibid.

CHAPTER 16
DIFFERENTIATING BETWEEN DEMONS AND EMOTIONS

1. Strong's Concordance, s.v. "*kilyah*," accessed April 24, 2017, https://www.blueletterbible.org/lang/Lexicon/Lexicon.cfm ?strongs=H3629&t=KJV.

CHAPTER 17
WAGING WAR THAT WINS

1. Helps Word-Studies, s.v. "*anthistémi*," Bible Hub, accessed June 8, 2017, http://biblehub.com/greek/436.htm.

CONNECT WITH US!

CHARISMA HOUSE

(Spiritual Growth)

f Facebook.com/CharismaHouse

🐦 @CharismaHouse

📷 Instagram.com/CharismaHouse

SILOAM

(Health)

📌 Pinterest.com/CharismaHouse

MODERN ENGLISH VERSION

(Bible)

www.mevbible.com